David Headon is a cultural consultant and historian. He is Advisor on the Centenary of Canberra and Advisor to Senator Kate Lundy.

Andrew MacKenzie is a landscape architect and Assistant Professor of Design at the University of Canberra.

CANBERRA RED

Stories from the bush capital

Edited by David Headon
and Andrew MacKenzie

ALLEN&UNWIN
SYDNEY • MELBOURNE • AUCKLAND • LONDON

First published in 2013

The extract from Judith Wright's *Fourth Quarter* is reproduced courtesy of Meredith McKinney & ETT Imprint, Sydney.

All attempts have been made to locate the owners of copyright material. If you have any information in that regard please contact the publisher at the address below.

Allen & Unwin
83 Alexander Street
Crows Nest NSW 2065
Australia
Phone: (61 2) 8425 0100
Email: info@allenandunwin.com
Web: www.allenandunwin.com

Cataloguing-in-Publication details are available from the National Library of Australia
www.trove.nla.gov.au

ISBN 978 1 74331 5 835 (pb)
ISBN 978 1 74331 5 965 (hb)

Jacket and internal design by Lisa White
Jacket photograph by Andrew MacKenzie
Set in 12/17 pt Minion Pro by Bookhouse, Sydney
Printed in Australia by Ligare Pty Ltd, Sydney

10 9 8 7 6 5 4 3 2 1

MIX
Paper from responsible sources
FSC® C011613
FSC www.fsc.org

The paper this book is printed on is in accordance with the rules of the Forest Stewardship Council®. The FSC® promotes environmentally responsible, socially beneficial and economically viable management of the world's forests.

CONTENTS

PREFACE

David Headon and Andrew MacKenzie

Canberra 'Red' is synonymous with the bush capital. First forged at the Yarralumla Brickworks in the 1920s, this fine brick would go on to serve the Canberra community's building aspirations for much of the twentieth century, earning its connotations of style, creativity, quality, solidity and, above all, longevity. The Red, an archetype of the facades that dominate old Canberra suburbs north and south of the lake today, was made to last.

As the title of this centenary collection of essays about the national capital, we found it irresistible.

Seventeen authors were asked to consider today's Canberra through the lens of their own experience of the city and what they have learned from a century of change, growth and realisation. All bring their expertise, philosophical stance and personal beliefs to the task, as they highlight particular individuals, events and ideas in order to provide fresh insights into a city just one hundred years in the making. You will see how the best intentions of past plans and ambitions about Canberra have at times been showcased, at times subverted—so that what we have at present is inevitably modified by what could have been and what still might be. Authors comment on the critical issues facing this and other cities today.

The book is about the bush capital, its compelling history and environment, and the people who continue to shape and re-shape it. Like every other city, it is unique. Opportunities and challenges exist in its structures and setting, culture and vibrant community life—and the rich range of myths and narratives that have brought it into being, but are yet to confirm its special place in the collective imagination of the nation. The problem, of course, rests not with the city but the nation.

We are now in the first quarter of the twenty-first century, a precise one hundred years after Canberra came into being through the ambition and vision of its Federation founders. Back then, the city was conceived as the direct result of a mightily progressive international design competition to build a young democratic nation's capital. Canberra is one of a handful of planned capitals around the world, and undoubtedly the world's most beautiful capital city in the landscape. Unlike most other cities, it was imagined and represented even before a single road or building had been constructed. Marion Mahony Griffin's sixteen exquisite competition renderings of 1911–12 translating Walter's iconic vision, including the panoramic view from Mount Ainslie, depict a place of remarkable formal harmony. She effortlessly unifies the dichotomies perceived between bush and city, the uninhabitable and habitable, nature and human settlement.

Over the last century, grand architectural gestures of political and cultural institutions steadily emerged that gave shape to the capital, often inciting rather than solving the question of national significance. Today, whole slabs of the city contain patchworks of suburban streets lined with humble government housing or 'govvies', swallowed by towering iron barks and sinewy brittle gums. Some locals still believe that the city has yet to provide the urbanity sorely missed by public servants in Canberra's past when they were dragooned into relocating to the Limestone Plains from Melbourne and Sydney, first in the 1920s and then in much larger numbers in the 1960s.

These days, Canberra proudly boasts the advantages and benefits of an urban community without the diseconomies of scale and cost. However, much of the focus of topical discussion and debate continues to focus on the city's role and functions as the national capital. Canberra is home to Australia's major research and cultural institutions, and much of the knowledge that has emerged has become nationally and globally significant. Canberra has not only housed these organisations, it has also on many occasions been the specific case study, the field laboratory for important critical enquiry. This book takes its place within that research tradition, asking how the capital is embodied, exerted, reinforced and reproduced in the minds of the Canberra community.

We hope that *Canberra Red* will be a catalyst prompting readers to contemplate how Canberra has matured beyond its original conception as an ideal garden city hybrid experiment. While the city in the future will continue to be an important subset of our national identity, as the result of its history, design significance and set of symbolic roles, that future is certain to be contested. Part-problem, part-mystery and part-discovery, it belongs to all Australians. This custodian responsibility is at once heritage challenge and profound cultural opportunity.

P.1 The Yarralumla Brickworks manufactured the Canberra red brick from the founding of the city until the late 1970s.

1

LEARNING TO LIVE ON THE LIMESTONE PLAINS

Kate Rigby

Up Red Hill:

A story of stone and Sky

According to my trusty geological guidebook compiled by Douglas Finlayson[1], the stone that predominates on Red Hill itself is a type of 'hornfels', rock that was baked and recrystallised around 417 to 408 million years ago. Within the vast timescale of the Earth history of this area, however, Canberra's foundations began to be laid down around 470 million years ago with the formation of a continental crust along the eastern margin of the ancient mega-continent of Gondwana, long before Australia had separated from Antarctica. The deep ocean sediments that were deposited on this crust were compressed over time to create what geologists have termed the Adaminaby, Nungar and Foxlow beds (c. 470–440 million years ago), in which the fossilised remains of some of Earth's earliest life forms have been found. These ancient rock beds are still visible in the cutting at the Corin Dam carpark in Namadgi National Park, while the similarly primordial

Pittman Formation (460–445 million years ago) peeks through near Queanbeyan at Molonglo Gorge. Two cycles of tectonic activity between about 443 and 430 million years ago caused these rock formations to be folded and faulted. Further sediments were later laid down, as various areas of the land surface rose and subsided, baked and eroded, and were, at various times, covered by water or volcanic lava. The layering that tells the story of these ancient transformations can be seen in many places around Canberra. One of the most fascinating in the city itself is the 'unconformity' that was revealed by the State Circle road cutting around Capital Hill. John Cameron has described his delight 'as a teenage rockhound' to behold in the 'divided rocks that dipped at such different angles from each other' a gap in geological time. This unconformity was formed, he explains:

> *when a layer of mud was deposited under the sea and compacted and heated to form the State Circle Slate around 440 million years ago. It was then raised up above the surface of the sea and eroded. About ten million years later, it sank down again below the surface of the sea and a layer of sand was deposited on top of it, but not parallel with, not on the same inclination or surface as the original sediments. These were later compacted to form the Camp Hill Sandstone.*[2]

Up until about 350 million years ago, the Canberra region continued to be highly volatile as its topography was remoulded many times over by powerful tectonic forces unleashed by the convergence of the Australian and Pacific plates. This prompted several cycles of volcanic activity, including the eruptions of Mount Pleasant around 425–424 million years ago, that formed the dactite that was used in combination with Black Mountain sandstone to such good effect by early European settlers in the building of St John's Church during the 1840s. It was also around 425 million years ago that the limestone was laid down that lent the Canberra region its first whitefella name: the Limestone Plains, so called for the outcrops on the Acton Peninsula that were encountered by the first British settler in this area, Joshua Moore, who, in 1824, adopted a local Aboriginal term, *Ngambra*, believed to mean 'meeting place', to name his property 'Canberry'. Looking down from the eroded hills that once spewed fire and ash and molten rock far and wide towards the lake that now lies in state upon the plains, you can discern the contours of the rift that was created by the alternation of tectonic movements and weatherborne erosion. It was this rift formation, bounded on all sides by fault lines, which lured the Molonglo River to make its way across what would become the first Australians' *Ngambra*, and which, much much later, also conditioned the Y-plan for the city of Canberra.

Turning to gaze upon the mountain ranges beyond the Canberra hills and plains, you can see the legacy of another weird phenomenon that took place between around 435 and 380 million years ago: the burbling up of molten rock from the mid to lower levels of the Earth's crust, probably guided by pre-existing deep faults and shear zones, to form mushroom-like 'plutons' as it cooled and hardened. The erosion of the softer rock into which these plutons had intruded subsequently exposed them, creating the spectacular granite outcrops that dominate the landscape of the Brindabellas and Tinderrys. Rock shelters in what is now Namadgi National Park provided seasonal accommodation for the Ngunnawal, Wolgal and Ngarigo peoples, whose long residence there, as evidenced by surviving stone artefacts, ceremonial stone circles and rock art, can be traced back at least 21 000 years, while narrow crevices in the weathered granite of the higher peaks continue to shelter the aestivating Bogong moths on which these peoples once feasted during large ceremonial gatherings in the warmer months. These days, if you go to Namadgi at the right time of year, during a good season you might be lucky enough to get a taste of roasted Bogong moth, suitably prepared by an Aboriginal guide—something that was unknown when I was growing up in Canberra at a time when knowledge of Aboriginal culture in this region, at least among white kids like me, let alone recognition of Aboriginal dispossession, was generally minimal, at best.

From about 395 million years ago, tectonic activity moved away to the east and west of the Canberra region, and by 370 million years ago most crustal rocks were in place. Changes nonetheless continued, including three periods of uplift and erosion between the late Permian and the early Cenozoic era. During this period, the continent of Gondwana drifted south to far colder climes, and 'for about 100 million years in the late Paleozoic era the Canberra region and Namadgi National Park were in an elevated position and subjected to glaciation and large-scale denudation of the landscape'[3], devastating the plant and animal life that had in the meantime evolved and colonised this area: a reminder that the stories of stone and sky, geology and climate, and the fate of life, are intimately interlinked. More congenial conditions for living critters, among whom those charismatic dinosaurs were numbered, came with the Triassic and Jurassic eras, but it was not until the Australian continent broke away from Antarctica and began its slow but inexorable journey to the north around 55 million years ago that temperatures really began to heat up, while nonetheless oscillating between warmer and cooler periods as the pattern of glacials and interglacials set in. Although Earth was gradually growing more quiescent in this area, Australia's northward drift engendered new tectonic stresses, prompting a volcanic eruption in Namadgi around 18 million years ago and, between about 10 and 5 million years ago, bringing Lake George into being by cutting off the outlets of the streams that traversed the plain beneath the escarpment. Minor earthquakes still rattle the Canberra region from time to time, such as the one on 3 October 2003 measuring 1.4, which had its epicentre right under Red Hill. Erosional processes also continue to scour the land, especially in those areas where deforestation has exposed the thin and fragile soils of this geologically ancient land.

Up Red Hill is also a good place to look to the heavens and watch the moon rise. Friends of mine come here to do just that, with a picnic tea and a bottle of wine, whenever they can on the night of full moon. Out near Tidbinbilla, though, at the Canberra Deep Space Communication Complex, opened in 1965 and the only NASA tracking station still in operation in Australia, astronomers peer into far more distant regions of the heavens, reconstructing the cosmic prehistory of the creation of this place by physical forces of immense power and enduring mystery. To lift your eyes from stone to sky is to reckon with timescales of even more mind-boggling magnitude, for deep space is also deep time, stretching back almost 14 billion years to when astronomers currently believe our universe was birthed. The realm of space remains no less dynamic than that of Earth, and our planet feels its impact in many ways: most dramatically so in occasional meteor strikes, such as that which is thought to have brought about the mass extinction event at the end of the Cretaceous era (around 65 million years ago) that did for the dinosaurs. In more quotidian ways, too, every place on Earth—including this young city—remains at the mercy of what comes to us, since time immemorial, from the sky. For instance, that wondrous sunshine, upon which the very emergence and survival of Earth's diverse organic life forms is dependent; the gracious alternation of day and night, to which the biorhythms of virtually all land creatures are attuned; and the pattern of the seasons and the vagaries of the weather, which govern seedtime and harvest, flourishing and withering, the world over—something that those who live cocooned in air-conditioned buildings forget at their peril.

Climate, too, has its history, and that history has at crucial moments been shaped by the dynamic interaction of Earth and sky. Among the factors that are now known to influence our climate are the 100 000-year cycle governed by Earth's elliptical orbit around the Sun; the 42 000 year cycle arising from the tilt of Earth's axis; the 22 000 year cycle pertaining to Earth's wobble on its axis; and, less predictably, irregularities in sunspot activity and alterations in the chemical make-up of the lower layers of Earth's atmosphere. Extending up to a mere 140 kilometres from the ground, this is the 'great aerial ocean'[4], by whose grace we live and breathe and have our being. In the past, Earth's atmosphere has primarily been affected by the mix of gases produced by plant and animal life and Earth's own exhalations, including periodic volcanic eruptions. While the particulates spewed into the atmosphere by major eruptions lower surface temperatures, the carbon dioxide that is released along with the magma and ash can subsequently raise them. This happened, for example, at the end of the Permian period, around 251 million years ago, when a spate of volcanic eruptions apparently precipitated a 6° Celsius rise in average global temperatures, which, in conjunction with the catastrophic immediate impact of these eruptions, resulted in the abrupt extinction of some 95 per cent of all species then in existence.

These days, of course, it is primarily industrial pollutants that are messing with Earth's atmosphere. Fluorocarbon pollution, for instance, has thinned Earth's protective ozone layer, allowing increased levels of ultraviolet radiation to beam down upon vulnerable organic life forms, especially at higher latitudes (including southern Australia). Chlorofluorocarbons have now been phased out by governmental legislation, and the ozone layer is expected to recover in time, while particulate pollution, which tends to lower temperatures, is also being brought under control in many places. The latter is a mixed blessing, however, as it means that 'global dimming' will no longer act as a moderating influence on the current increase in global temperatures, which, as we know with as much certainty as science can ever provide, is largely being driven by industrialised humanity's ever-increasing combustion of fossil fuels, combined with ongoing destruction of the forests that we now need more than ever to soak up the excess carbon dioxide that we are producing and to sustain Earth's threatened biodiversity. Despite their relatively high uptake of alternative energy sources and the readiness of many to recycle, ride bikes and vote Green, Canberrans, with their literally high-powered lifestyle and predominant car culture, are contributing considerably more per capita than most people around the world to anthropogenic climate change. In some respects, they might also be especially vulnerable to its impacts. While much of Australia is likely to see an intensification of the extreme weather events that this 'land of droughts and flooding rains' has long been prone to, there are indications that the Canberra region, along with other major cities in the mid latitudes (Perth, Adelaide, Melbourne and Sydney), might heat up more rapidly and dramatically than elsewhere in Australia. This, at any rate, is what happened at the end of the last Ice Age, around 20 000 years ago. According to the International Panel on Climate Change, predicting the regional impacts of global warming remains an uncertain affair. But if this historical pattern is repeated, it is likely to make events like the firestorm of 2003, and the intense dry period that led up to it, a more common occurrence.

If Canberrans are to learn to live more sustainably in a perilously warming world, I believe they would do well to look to the example of those peoples who succeeded in weathering several major climate changes in the past to craft a flourishing *modus vivendi* in this place.

Down by the river: the making and taking of Kamberri country

Pialligo is where my mother and I used to come on summer Saturdays to buy the kinds of fruit, fresh from the orchard, that didn't grow on the trees in our garden. Some fruit and vegetables are still cultivated here, and there are nurseries in abundance as well. For, as the Chinese who established the first market gardens here discovered, this is where you will find the most fertile soil in Canberra. This is largely thanks to the river that started flowing this way after the rift was formed, making these plains a welcoming place, flush with tucker, for the Aboriginal peoples who gave it one of the names by which it is still known: Molonglo, 'the thunderer'; so called, perhaps, for its boisterous behaviour in full spate, a tributary of the Murrumbidgee, and so part of the hard-pressed Murray–Darling system that waters so much of south-eastern Australia.

The generations of stone tools found on a sandy rise above the river at Pialligo indicate that this was an especially important seasonal camping ground, where many people stayed for long periods. 'They can only have done so,' as Bill Gammage observes, 'if their food supply was certain and convenient. Within a few hundred metres, a shorter distance than most of us travel to the supermarket, swamp, river, plain, hill and forest were handy'[5], each well stocked with a distinctive range of comestibles. On the basis of descriptions provided by explorers, settlers and early land surveyors, backed up by recent research into Aboriginal land-use practices from other parts of Australia, Gammage has reconstructed a picture of the heartland of *Ngambra*, 'meeting place' of the various peoples that the new settlers referred to collectively as the Kamberri[6], as it might have been in the early nineteenth century. Tracing a path from the campus of the Australian National University at Acton along Sullivans Creek to the Molonglo, then upriver to where the airport is now situated, Gammage maps a mixed landscape of swampy flats and flowing water, grassy paddocks with woodland on the ridges, encircled by the forested hillsides of Black Mountain, Mount Pleasant and Mount Ainslie, opening out onto a broad plain reaching to undulating open forest, and forming a patchwork with discrete places for hunting, collecting, celebrating and camping. Among the foods provided by this eminently 'nourishing terrain'[7], Gammage lists *typha* reeds, yams, native artichokes, grass orchid bulbs, swans, ducks and other waterbirds, eggs, fish, crayfish, shellfish, water rats, snakes, goannas, platypus, emu, plains turkey, quail, kangaroos, wallabies, possums, small marsupials and the lerp insect manna found on ribbon gum. In addition, there were numerous medicines to be found here, and abundant materials for making tools, weapons, clothing, dilly bags and shelters, and, as already mentioned, in the rocky upper reaches of the Brindabellas, the tasty moths that drew together large numbers of people from neighbouring countries for trade and talk and ceremony and feasting.

1.1 Kayakers on the Murrumbidgee River.

'If you want to know where our sites are just look around you,' B.J. Cruse, an Aboriginal officer with the local land council in Eden, told historian Mark McKenna, 'we like the same spots you do'[8]. It was this shared liking for certain kinds of places, in combination with the profound differences in the way those places would be treated, that proved disastrous for Aboriginal people, especially in the less arid regions of south-eastern Australia. This was certainly true in the case of the Canberra area. Maintaining the land as an Aboriginal dwelling place, Gammage stresses, requires a great deal of knowledge, skill and hard work, and those '[p]laces where people gathered needed special care, otherwise they couldn't gather. For that reason they attracted Europeans. All over Australia Europeans first located on the heartlands Aborigines had made most carefully'. In Kamberri country, these included a major corroborree site on the Molonglo River at Acton, which was appropriated by John Joshua Moore's overseer in 1824, and the sandy rise upriver at Pialligo that afforded a cool, soft and dry warm-weather campsite, which Robert Campbell's stockman James Ainslie claimed the following year. The first resident landholder was James Macpherson at Acton, who called his property 'Springbank' after the water source on the Molonglo flats that never ran dry.

Along with their plants, animals, diseases and new regimes of land use, the colonisers also brought a set of assumptions about the natural world in general, and that of Australia in particular, which contrasted starkly with Aboriginal understandings. Back in Europe, the Romantic movement that swept Britain and Germany around 1800 had revalued the natural world as a locus of the holy. Something of this Romantic sensibility can be glimpsed in the letters of Terrence Aubrey Murray, who acquired Frances Mowatt's 'Yarralumla' property in 1836. Describing a difficult journey back to the Limestone Plains from Tumut through snow-covered mountains and flooded rivers in the winter of 1842, Murray tells his sister that he was 'repaid for my trouble by the grand and sublime appearance of those noble hills in their frozen and wintry garb . . . The mountains are grander than I can describe in their pristine state . . . I wish you could see them.'[9] While aesthetically pleasing for some, and even worthy of protection for a minority, the colonial Earth was nonetheless primarily of interest to European settlers for its pecuniary value. Samuel Shumack, son of the first selector on the Limestone Plains, for example, observes approvingly in his memoirs that Robert Campbell recognised that 'this unknown land under proper management would, in the future, become one of the greatest producing emporiums of the world'[10]. As an 'emporium', Earth is construed as a source of goods to be bought and sold: formerly the seal skins made Campbell's fortune, by the 1820s these were replaced mainly by fleeces for the woollen mills back in England; later it would also be wheat and meat, while today, of course, it is above all minerals, including the coal exports to China that are now helping to destabilise the climate.

Over the course of the nineteenth century, European settlement on and around the Limestone Plains significantly altered the ecology of this region, as well as devastating the lives of those peoples who had moulded it sustainably for millennia. By 1850, under the hard hoofs and intensive grazing of the settlers' sheep and cattle, the swathes of succulent purplish-green kangaroo grass, carefully cultivated by Aboriginal burning, had given way to less nutritious wallaby grass and spear grass. Some timbered areas had been cleared, with bullock tracks on sloping ground causing erosion and the formation of small creeks, which washed topsoil downhill, clogging waterways; and some animal species were beginning to decline as they were shot in ever greater numbers either for sport, for the table, or because they grazed the settlers' crops or raided their orchards. Whereas the Indigenous landholders had developed a mobile and flexible mode of dwelling well adapted to the unpredictability of the climate and generally poor soils of this region, the newcomers sought to impose forms of land use that had been developed under very different environmental conditions. This misfit proved particularly problematic for the smallholders who selected land here from the 1860s and continued to plough on, working the land in a manner that assumed a regular cycle of four seasons, as well as considerably deeper and richer soil, with the result that their labours were frequently foiled by environmental conditions that defied their expectations. Selectors were required to clear and fence their land, so deforestation accelerated from the 1860s, exacerbating erosion and

1.2 The Molonglo River in flood before the completion of the Scrivener Dam.

putting further pressure on wildlife. Moreover, while several native species, such as emu, bustard, koala and kangaroo rat, were hunted to extinction locally, a number of introduced ones, such as Scotch thistle and rabbits, soon proved pestilential.

Early settlers, here as elsewhere in Australia, frequently relied upon Aboriginal cooperation, knowledge and labour, and there is evidence of a degree of co-existence and, in some cases, such as that of Murray and his manager Stuart Mowle, possibly even friendship between some newcomers and the locals in the Canberra area. By the early 1860s, however, disease and dispossession appear to have already taken a heavy toll. While a small number of Aboriginal stockmen, whose horsemanship, tracking and other skills were held in high regard by pastoralists, continued to work on some of the larger estates up until at least the 1880s, many of the surviving Indigenous population were dispersed, some joining larger groups elsewhere in the region, while others went onto mission stations. A few endeavoured to make themselves self-sufficient, after the European fashion, on small farms that were provided by the authorities to 'well-behaved' Aboriginal families. Among the new wave of settlers, there were some, such as Samuel Shumack, whose family arrived on the Limestone Plains in 1856, who railed against the 'vile treatment' of 'the natives' by 'white despoilers' and regretted their passing with the death of Queen Nellie Hamilton, mistakenly believed to be the 'last of her tribe', in 1897. Indeed, Samuel Shumack describes Nellie as 'a very intelligent woman', who 'was honest and truthful', and even gives her a voice of protest in his memoirs, recalling how she once responded to being hauled off to the Queanbeyan gaol for drunkenness with the defiant observation:

> *Yah, you have a lot of big rich men over there that should be in there. You come and take our land and kill our game and let us starve, and if we take a sheep or kill a calf you shoot us or put us in gaol. You bring your disease and give it to us—we had nothing like that until you came and stole our land—you give us rotten blanket and bad rum.*[11]

Nonetheless, the myth that the Aboriginal population had 'died out', and that it was the squatters who were to blame, was a convenient one for the new smallholders, for, unlike on the big pastoral properties, there was no place for 'natives' on the selectors' farms. Nor, it seems, was there to be any place for the first Australians in the new nation's federal capital: 'After the Australian Capital Territory (ACT) was established in 1911, the Aboriginal Protection Board forced all its Aboriginal residents to move to Edgerton Mission Station, 16 kilometres East of Yass'[12], from whence they were later moved onto other missions in Yass, Wallaga Lake, Cowra, Narrandera and Tumut. In the 1920s, however, at least one local family, that of Roddy Williams, was still camping on Red Hill, and Roddy also maintained a room in a local working man's hostel. Perhaps he was among the Aboriginal labourers employed in the construction of Parliament House, the official opening of which in 1927 was attended by two Wiradjuri 'clever men'—John Noble, who had been working as a shepherd in the district, and Jimmy Clements. Today, in addition to many Aboriginal residents from other parts of Australia, there are hundreds of people, identifying mainly as Ngunnawal, Ngarigo or Wiradjuri, with ancestral ties to this area living in Canberra, and their traditional lifeways are commemorated in the Bogong moth sculptures that grace the ground between the Australian Institute of Aboriginal and Torres Strait Islander Studies and the National Museum of Australia on the Acton Peninsula. Meanwhile, the lifeways of the pastoralists and farmers who appropriated their land has itself been displaced by the transformation of the Limestone Plains into the site of Australia's capital city.

Under Capital Hill:
The construction of a designer city

Kurrajong Hill, as it was known when it was still part of William and Elizabeth Klensendorlffe's property, is one of the Gura Bung Dhaura hills and it was a traditional campsite of the Ngunnawal on their regular journeys between Black Mountain and Tuggeranong, via Stirling Ridge, the Gap, Red Hill and Mugga Mugga. According to Ann Gugler, at least one Ngunnawal family, the Carrolls, were still camping there into the 1930s. By that time, a succession of politicians, surveyors and workmen had also pitched their tents on Kurrajong, as the construction of Australia's capital city finally got underway. Walter Burley Griffin intended this to be the site of a building called the Capitol, housing the national archives as well as being a place of popular assembly dedicated to commemorating creative, scholarly and sporting achievements embodying the spirit of the nation. Significantly, Griffin wished the Capitol to be exalted above the Parliament building, sited below on Camp Hill, symbolising his democratic vision of the new nation as a country in which the everyday business of government was guided and illuminated by the spiritual ideals of the people.

Regrettably, perhaps, the Capitol was never built, and the site earmarked as a place of popular entertainment at the opposite end of the land axis, Griffin's 'Casino', became the location instead of a

1.3 View along Ainslie Avenue towards Mount Ainslie prior to the construction of the Canberra Centre.

dour War Memorial. The extraordinary Parliament House that now literally occupies Capital Hill does nonetheless accord with aspects of the Griffin vision, as well as exemplifying some of the 'unconformities' characterising the construction of Canberra as a whole. Nestling within, rather than built atop, the hill, it embodies Griffin's concept of a parliamentary building that symbolised the democratic ideal of government as serving the people, rather than lording it over the land.

For all that, though, this hill is clearly not what it once was. Gone is the grassy woodland, which John Cameron recalls as a rough kind of place in the 1960s. Littered with grog bottles and porno magazines left by the residents of the single working men's hostel then sited there, it was home also to sundry non-human critters, such as the stone curlew who is said to have been seen lamenting the loss of its habitat and companions when the scrub was cleared in favour of the neatly trimmed lawn that now decorates the hilltop. In the course of gutting its innards, construction workers revealed that at the heart of Capital Hill there lies 'the greatest degree of discordance in any known exposure of the unconformity,' which, Cameron observes, 'is of geological curiosity as well as metaphorical significance'[13]. In my view, a degree of unconformity characterises not only the new Parliament House, which both respects and refunctionalises the site, but also the city that surrounds this hollowed-out hill.

'As a public landscape,' James Weirick observed in 1988, 'Canberra has strange distortions of meaning and sense, there is a confusion of messages, with odd lacunae and complete silences'[14]. I too have written elsewhere of such mixed messages, pointing in particular to the contradictory tendencies that can be traced within the Griffin plan itself, between, on the one hand, respectful attunement to the materially pre-given and, on the other, the modernist impulse to remake the real in accordance with an abstract ideal, transcending the peculiarities of place. The strictly geometrical shaping of urban space through the arrangement of roads, significant buildings and functionally discrete zones, for example, accords with the neoclassical conventions of the City Beautiful movement and exemplifies modernist universalism. Unusually, though, the major and minor axes of the central city are aligned with the pre-existing topographical features of the site, namely the river and the surrounding hills. Because the focal points of the city's radial avenues are not the conventional arches, obelisks or monumental buildings of the City Beautiful, but rather hills and mountains, your gaze is continuously being drawn beyond the humanly crafted townscape towards the skyline of the surrounding countryside (a principle that was betrayed in the erection of a large telecommunications tower on Black Mountain, against strong local opposition, in the 1970s). In this sense, Griffin 'willed his plan the servant not the master/of a chosen place,' as Michael Thwaites puts it in his 'Psalm for an Artificial City'.[15]

This responsiveness to the lie of the land nonetheless sits somewhat unconformably with the emphatically neoclassical nature of the design, which effectively obliterates any remaining traces of pastoral, not to mention Aboriginal inhabitation of this area, valorising the universal in a distinctly European guise and evoking comparisons of Canberra with seven-hilled Rome. The Griffins evidently valued geometrical design as expressive of a primordial language of nature, as seen for example in crystal formation. There is debate as to what kind of symbolic significance the Griffins attached to this, but sacred geometry was much discussed in the spiritualist movements in which some of their associates in Chicago were involved, and with which they themselves were later affiliated,[16] as well as carrying more secular democratic connotations. In either case, it is clear that in the Griffin vision, landscape was valued for far more than its picturesque views. Rather, the democratic aspirations that the Griffins optimistically attributed to the new Australian nation were for them necessarily tied to the re-harmonisation of society and nature. 'By using its topographical features as axial determinants and visual foci,' as Chris Vernon observes, 'the Griffins "monumentalized" the future city's physical site.'[17]

Yet the pull of the picturesque, coupled with the privileging of human action over other-than-human agency, proved irresistible, even for the Griffins. Tellingly, in his *Report Explanatory*, Griffin refers to the site as 'an irregular amphitheatre', with the 'distant mountain ranges, sun reflecting, forming the back scene of the theatrical whole'[18]. Here, the landscape is relegated to the level of scenery, thereby placing the natural environment at the disposal of exclusively human agents, whose interactions are implicitly constituted as the only show in town. The stately setting deemed necessary for the drama of democratic government, moreover, demanded the sacrifice of the fickle river, whose ways were far too unruly to be encompassed within the Griffins' geometric ideal. In fairness, it should be noted that the labile river was probably always going to go. Prone periodically to flooding the Canberra plain, the Molonglo dwindled to a series of muddy waterholes in drought years. Clearly, a more dependable and demure body of water was called for as the centrepiece of this neoclassical capital. The Griffins' solution called for the creation of three formal basins, flanked by two larger and more natural-looking lakes. Here, too, the tension between respectful attunement and modernist remaking is evident. While Vernon suggests the lakes were intended to 'take on the character of a naturally occurring wetland', the construction of the geometrically contained architectural pools would have necessitated moving over a million cubic yards of earth.

As it turned out, the Griffins' concept for Canberra's liquid heart was later ditched in favour of an unambiguously picturesque design. Completed only in 1964, the lake that bears Griffin's name simulates nature by following, more or less, the contours of the floodplain around its irregular edge. By this time, the whole Griffin plan had been substantially amended, partly for practical and financial reasons, but also in accordance with a succession of differing visions for the city pursued by a succession of town planners, following Griffin's disgruntled departure from the scene in 1920. These were in particular the Garden City ideal favoured by Griffin's immediate successor, John Sulman, and subsequently, the British Modernist model adopted by the National Capital Development Commission (NCDC), established by the Menzies government in 1958.

For the proponents of the Garden City movement, landscape features not so much as a scenic backdrop, but as a dwelling place by incorporating aspects of the rural into the urban environment in the guise of private gardens and public parks, where, to cite John Sulman, 'one can roam at will, families can picnic, and cattle and sheep can graze'[19]. The Griffins were sympathetic to this ideal, and it informed their design for the suburbs. Griffin also established an arboretum to facilitate the reafforestation of the hillsides. They nonetheless envisaged a relatively built-up downtown area, including some medium-density housing in European-style apartment blocks with internal courtyards. Instead, under Sulman's influence, Canberra became a stolidly suburban town of burgeoning bungalows, from whence, thanks to the NCDC's enthusiasm for the automobile, the city's generally well-heeled, white-collared citizens sallied forth, in the main, by private car. At the same time that roads and freeways were being laid down with planned abandon, however, the whole town was becoming ever leafier. Owing to a massive tree-planting campaign initiated in 1913 and continuing on a smaller scale right up to the present, Canberra is one of the few cities in the world where urban development has dramatically increased tree cover. Although most of the earlier plantings were of exotic deciduous varieties deemed hardy enough to cope with the frosty winters of these wind-blown high plains, the newer suburbs that grew rapidly during the 1970s, in strict accordance with the NCDC's 'Y-plan', featured indigenous street plantings as well as increasing numbers of native gardens on private blocks. The NCDC also developed an 'open space' system that ensured the retention of ribbons of pre-existing grassy woodland and open forest threaded throughout Canberra's residential areas.

Canberra's open space has been compromised in recent years by the insidious creep of housing up hillsides and the expansion of roadways, such as the hotly contested Gungahlin Drive Extension that took a bite out of the O'Connor Ridge parkland, while ever more of the farmland on the city's fringes has been sacrificed to suburbs. As it reaches its centenary, Canberra nonetheless continues to provide habitat for a diversity of wildlife, including an extraordinary profusion of birds, along with the Bogong moths that have taken to invading the new Parliament House on their annual migration, and it also affords its human residents ready access to grassy woodland, forests and waterways, both within and beyond the city's perimeters. Once carrying derisory connotations, Canberra's identity as Bush Capital is now seen as something to celebrate, as do Ian Fraser and Peter Marsack, for example, in their beautiful natural history of the Canberra region. All this, however, is threatened, not only by urban expansion but, more grievously, if less visibly, by global warming.

As Mark Tredinnick observes, 'the weather we have known—the weather that gave rise to the vivid and teeming, immaculate world in which the human species evolved, and all that it has dreamed and learnt and lost and made—is passing away. The weather of the Holocene is dying out' and, along with it, a large and growing percentage of those

1.4 The Red Hill Carousel opened in 1964.

myriad species into whose midst ours came to be—'and the weather of the Anthropocene "is turning nasty"'[20]. Just how nasty it becomes can probably still be influenced by the political decisions that are taken now and for a few (but only a few) more years to come, at various levels and in various forums around the world, including right here, under Capital Hill in Australia's federal parliament. In this respect, the ACT Legislative Assembly, spurred on by strong community activism, has been leading the way, introducing the most ambitious greenhouse gas reduction targets in the country in 2010.

At this perilous historical juncture, moreover, something is stirring in Canberra, pointing beyond emissions targets towards a more profound socio-ecological shift: a prophetic imagination, which promises to bring together the deep democracy envisioned by the Griffins with the deep sustainability that we so badly need in the present. This prophetic imagination rarely gets a hearing in the flashy new Parliament House, but for a few nights in September 2010 it was given voice nearby, just down the way in Australia's gracious old parliamentary buildings, in the performance by Canberra's Chorus of Women of Glenda Cloughley's extraordinary story-song, *The Gifts of the Furies*[21]. Summoning the mythic figure of the Furies from Aeschylus' tragic drama, *The Oresteia*, who avenge crimes against mothers and Mother Earth, this performance prefigured the bitter harvest that continued greenhouse gas pollution is likely to reap, a foretaste of which was visited upon Canberra in 2003:

I'll bring drought and fire under filthy skies
I'll scorch the farmland and torch the forest
I'll raise the oceans drown the cities
I'll spare no human being

1.5 The Furies of Earth await the verdict of Ethos, Old Parliament House, 2010.

In *The Oresteia*, however, the Furies are ultimately persuaded to desist from their vengeful pursuit of Orestes, who had murdered his mother to avenge her murder of his father to avenge his murder of their daughter, who had been sacrificed to raise the winds that enabled the Greek fleet to set sail for their battle with Troy. This cycle of vengeance is broken in Aeschylus' play, the first extant courtroom drama in western history, by the intervention of the Goddess Athena, whose casting vote grants leniency to Orestes in order to avert civil war, at the same time as she institutes a new practice of honouring the life-giving agency of mothers and Earth within the city, transforming the Furies into the Eumenides, or 'Kindly Ones'. Similarly, *The Gifts of the Furies* envisages a reconciliation of the *logos* of urban civilisation with the ineluctable laws of Earth and Sky in the context of climate change; but in this case, the wisdom of Athena is accorded to the figure of Ethos, inspired by Tom Bass's sculpture of the 'spirit of the community', which stands outside the ACT Legislative Assembly on Civic Square. While the language that predominates among those who currently debate such practical policy issues as environmental river flows, public transportation and carbon pricing under Capital Hill remains largely locked into the human-centred and economistic mindset of those for whom the colonial Earth was little more than an 'emporium', it is to be hoped that enough of them will hearken in time to the prophetic voices that were raised in Old Parliament House, as well as in various other venues both before and since, in the performance of *The Gifts of the Furies*. Although these voices were human, they were singing of, and for, a far more inclusive community of life, when they closed with this pledge:

Gaia! We your people sing our promise
to turn the tide to harmony
of the mortal law of people and cities
and the immortal law of Earth and Sky

Gaia! We are the voice of our children's hope
We are the trust of creatures and plants
We the dreamers we the singers
Will never tire of telling you your gifts

How Canberra, and indeed the rest of Australia, fares in the next one hundred years will depend in no small measure on whether the people's representatives who meet in the Bush Capital come to join the Chorus of Women in upholding this promise.

Acknowledgements

Research towards 'Learning to Live on the Limestone Plains' was supported by a Visiting Fellowship with the Historical Research Centre of the National Museum of Australia.

Notes

1 Douglas M. Finlayson (compiler), 2008. *A Geological Guide to Canberra Region and Namadgi National Park*, Geological Society of Australia (ACT Division), Canberra, p. 70.
2 John Cameron, 'Beneath Capital Hill: The Unconformities of Place and Self' in Tredinnick, M. (ed.), 2003. *A Place on Earth: An Anthology of Nature Writing from Australia and North America.* UNSW Press, Sydney, pp. 55–63.
3 Finlayson, p. 70.

4 Tim Flannery, 2005. *The Weather Makers: The History and Future Impact of Climate Change*, Text Publishing, Melbourne, pp. 19–26.
5 Bill Gammage, 'Australia Under Aboriginal Land Management', *2003 Barry Andrews Memorial Lecture*. University College, ADFA, Canberra.
6 Ann Jackson-Nakano,'The Kamberri: A history from the records of Aboriginal families in the Canberra-Queanbeyan district and surrounds 1820–27, and historical overview 1928–2001', *Aboriginal History*, Weeweewaa History Series, vol. 1, Canberra.
7 Deborah Bird Rose, 1996. *Nourishing Terrains: Australian Aboriginal views of landscape and wilderness,* Australian Heritage Commission, Canberra.
8 Mark McKenna, 2002. *Looking for Blackfellas' Point: An Australian history of place,* UNSW Press, Sydney.
9 T.A. Murray, 1842. Letter to Anna, July 15 1842 in 'Papers of the Murray Family', NLA Ms. 545.
10 Samuel Shumack, 1967. *An Autobiography, or Tales and Legends of Canberra Pioneers*. J.E. and S. Shumack, (eds) Australian National University Press, Canberra.
11 Shumack, ibid.
12 Carl Brown, Dorothy Brown Dickson, Loretta Bell Halloran, Fred Monaghan, Tracey Phillips, Sandra Phillips Austin, Agnes Bulger Shea, and next of kin of the late Berth Bell Thorpe, 2007. *Stories of the Ngunnawal*, Journey of Healing (ACT) Inc, Canberra.
13 John Cameron, 'Beneath Capital Hill: The Unconformities of Place and Self', in Tredinnick, M. (ed.) 2003. *A Place on Earth: An anthology of nature writing from Australia and North America*, UNSW Press, Sydney, pp. 55–63.
14 James Weirick, 'The Griffins and Modernism', *Transition*, 1988, vol. 24, pp. 5–13.
15 Michael Thwaites, 1993. *The Honey Man and other Poems*, Trend Setting, Canberra.
16 P.R. Proudfoot, 1994. *The Secret Plan of Canberra*, UNSW Press, Sydney.
17 Chris Vernon, 'Canberra: Where Landscape is Pre-eminent', in Gordon, David (ed.) 2006. *Planning Twentieth Century Cities*, Routledge, New York, p. 134.
18 W.B. Griffn, 1913. *The Federal Capital: Report Explanatory of the Preliminary General Plan*, Department of Home Affairs, Melbourne, p. 3.
19 John Sulman, 1921. *An Introduction to the Study of Town Planning in Australia*, William Applegate Gullick, Sydney, p. 339.
20 Mark Tredinnick, 2011. *Australia's Wild Weather*, National Library of Australia, Canberra.
21 See Chapter 10, this volume.

2

THE LONG DINNER PARTY

Frank Moorhouse

'They clinked glasses and drank "to Bloomsbury on the Molonglo".'
From *Cold Light*, Frank Moorhouse

While researching my novel *Cold Light* set in Canberra mainly in the 1950s, I was interested in constructing a simple (and incomplete) timeline of the progressive-intellectual life of Canberra in the city's formative period, which, arbitrarily, I identify as from, say, 1914 when the Griffins moved to Australia until the 1950s and the establishment of the Australian National University (ANU), when the flow of influential newcomers to Canberra becomes a torrent.

I was tracking not only beliefs and behaviour which went against the then contemporary mores but which were also sometimes illegal, or almost illegal—homosexuality, cross-dressing, blasphemy, ownership or importation of any of the hundreds of books banned in Australia and any dalliance with, or commitment to, communism. Until the 1970s, Australia was a very repressed culture.

I imagine the Canberra conversational line beginning in Chicago's innovative architectural and planning community, the ideas of which travelled with the Griffins to Australia in 1914 when they came to implement their prize-winning plan. This began a stream of visitors and new thinking which included the English Bloomsbury Group and other reformist ideas carried by wanderers—public servants, and others who found themselves involved in the making of Canberra—who 'washed up' in Canberra.

The Griffins arrived to confront the area marked on the map known as the new Federal Capital Territory, where first settlers from the 1820s onwards occupied two small villages, Hall and Tharwa, and ten large station properties (together with some smaller ones). The larger stations were generally developed on a feudal pattern, with a Big House surrounded by a cluster of employees' cottages in close-knit, small-scale communities comparable to those in rural districts of Britain. This scattering of people had a social life but I am more interested in the new arrivals who came to build and shape the capital city.

I see this part of intellectual life of Canberra as a long dinner party.

I imagine that the first Canberra dinner parties occurred in 1914 when the Residency (then Canberra House), built for the Administrator of Canberra, was ready for occupation and when Yarralumla station homestead—a three-storey building intended as a residence for the Governor-General—had been taken over to house temporarily senior public servants with business in Canberra, and the newly arrived Walter and Marion Griffin. I would imagine that there would've been some mixing with invited graziers from the surrounding stations over dinner.

The lamb, pork and beef steaks butchered on the surrounding properties would've been excellent. There might have been a rabbit, some quail, and some wild duck, shot on the Molonglo River or Lake George. Despite the fact that the Federal Capital Territory had a prohibition of the sale of alcohol I choose to think that they felt that the law did not apply to them and they'd have drunk beer, Scotch, and perhaps even some French wine, and would've finished the meal with port around a roaring log fire.

Canberra House was occupied by Colonel David Miller, Canberra's first administrator, and his wife. Miller had moved from his tent on-site to occupy the first large, grand two-storey house built in the new capital. At this time, Canberra was a settlement of tents and huts, first in 'camps' and then in portable housing, and seven cottages for about 2000 labourers, tradesmen, and an elite group of engineers, architects, accountants, botanists, senior public servants, landscapers, foresters, and visiting politicians and journalists.

The dramatic central subject always present, acknowledged or not, at every one of those dinners parties was *how to build a new city*—a capital—and following closely behind this subject would've tumbled out the great Socratic existential question 'how should we live?' The answers had to begin, and were philosophically inherent, in the questions of how best to arrange the streets, how to use trees, how to employ local materials, how best to lay a sewer system, and how to ensure adequate safe water.

I can't help feeling that the arrival of the Griffins, Marion and Walter, changed the Canberra conversation—the Australian conversation. Together the Griffins were a lightning bolt of new ideas not only about how to build but also about how to live—they brought a new vocabulary—and it was then that the Canberra dinner party began, arguing about Canberra. They introduced the idea that a city could be intricately symbolic—they introduced the idea that a city could be a work of art.

Their ideas included the new theories of town planning, of planned living, of ways of avoiding the creation of slums and the effect that poor sanitation and housing had on the social wellbeing—the Garden City philosophies—how to live in cities without losing touch with nature. Even if some of the architects and engineers had come across the Garden City ideas in their reading, now they were talking with a couple who *practised* the philosophy, who had worked with Frank Lloyd Wright in Chicago, and who expounded it with the authority of the American accent.

The Garden City philosophy was about the creation of a harmonious combination of city and country, of dwelling house and garden. It is perhaps the most important thing that the Griffins brought to the making of Canberra—the streets were tree-lined using only one species of tree in any given street, with a centre nature strip and garden traffic islands, in wide 'motorways'; houses without front fences whose front lawns flowed out onto wide grassy footpaths.

We know that from the start Miller the Administrator and the Griffins argued hotly about the plan—how Canberra should look and what sort of example of modern good living would the capital give to Australia. Miller, a former Boer War officer and senior public servant, quickly became part of a conspiracy to disregard the Griffin Plan mostly on the grounds of extravagance—not aesthetics or principles of design.

Ideas abounded about houses—houses which met the requirements of the unfolding twentieth century—that is, they were to be servant-less (or at least servants were not intended to live in) and they were to be hygienic and healthy—sleep-outs were considered healthy for the children—with silent, indoor, flushing toilets, underground electricity and telephone lines, and streets suitable for the automobile and bus.

Kids should be able to walk to school. From the windows of every dwelling it would be possible to see the sky, experience the weather. Walter would have introduced his plans for a fireproof house. He may have ventured ideas of 'the natural house'—'a house that emerges as an aesthetic solution to the problems facing the architect while reflecting both the spirit of the nation and the ideal of domestic life'[1], according to Dustin Griffin, Professor of English at New York University and grandnephew of Walter Burley Griffin.

'The precincts developed for the first permanent housing in Canberra in the 1920s have matured into the most substantial and distinctive suburban environments inspired by the Garden City movement in Australia . . . No other Australian city boasts such an extensive set of self-consciously designed and controlled projects . . .' is how Peter Freeman, a conservation architect and planner, describes it.

The Griffins might have talked also about Hull House in Chicago, one of the first American 'settlement houses' which espoused social reform. Jill Roe, the biographer of Miles Franklin, and I both fancy that the Griffins would have met Miles Franklin there because she was visiting Chicago and had a strong interest in the settlement movement. They became friends around this time. The settlement movement beginning in the late 1880s in England and the United States advocated planning policies which would bring about societies where the rich and the poor lived more closely together in an interdependent community. The underlying aim, stated or not, was that this would raise the quality of life for the lower income groups by example, and by offering the underprivileged pathways to knowledge through adult education.

This movement began in Australia in 1908 and today traces of it lie behind Canberra's 'affordable housing' policies which are based on the idea that in a good society people of all income levels should be living among each other and not in class ghettos.

And maybe, later at night over port, the Griffins, especially Marion, would've thrown in some ideas from the thinking of the Theosophists and the anthroposophist Rudolph Steiner.

When asked about theosophy I can imagine Marion saying something like, 'the Theosophists think that we do best when we bring the universe, humanity and spiritual into relationships with each other'. Or she may have paraphrased the words of Antoine Faivre, who stated that 'the Theosophist dedicates his energy to discovering things visible and invisible, by examining nature in the smallest detail and believing that things are not just pieces of matter—they are living entities that surge and evolve with dynamic flows of energy and light'[2], and that good architecture and planning used these energies.

Some at the dinner party may have taken out their watches from their fob pockets and looked at the time.

Marion believed that symbols could speak to those who live among them. She accepted Steiner's proposition that the circle, triangle, crescent and square expressed the 'four ethers'. Steiner was also an early innovator in the use of concrete to achieve organic and spiritually expressive forms.

Perhaps some of this Canberra elite at dinner in one of the only two grand houses there in the paddocks of Canberra, surrounded by bushland and the wild winds of the plains, at times felt that they were a long way 'out of the loop', exiled from the artistic and intellectual centres of Australia and the world. Even now, in 2013, I've heard jokes about Canberra being a 'hardship posting'.

But also, those early Canberra intellectuals would, from time to time, have been brought back to a realisation that they were involved in a tremendously great experiment—that Canberra and the decisions they were making were part of *what was happening* intellectually in the world through the creation of this capital city. They had a rare, maybe unique, opportunity to shape living by using human intelligence to create a new symbolic city.

And then let's say, somewhere around the mid-1920s, Canberra began to look like a town with a permanent as well as an ever-changing population of about 6000—politicians who were there when parliament was sitting, visiting public servants, visiting experts, journalists who came and went. In 1925, the Hotel Canberra was now open for business followed by other hotels, the Brassey and the Kurrajong, bringing the new standards of hotel dining rooms, and in 1927 the Parliament House was opened; Manuka and Kingston were taking shape.

The Griffins left in 1921 defeated by interference. They remained in Australia and Miles Franklin is quoted by Roe as saying 'The poor man confessed to me his bitterness; is sorry he did not stay in the United States . . . The way he is persecuted and thwarted is shameful.'[3]

In the late 1920s another couple arrived—'washed up'—in Canberra from the distant outside world of arts and ideas—Charles and Ruth Lane Poole.

Charles was appointed head of forestry in Canberra (taking over from Thomas Weston) and their first dinner party would've been in one of Canberra's new grand houses—Westridge House, designed by Harold Desbrowe-Annear, a Melbourne friend of Ruth—a fine Tudor-style, Arts and Crafts half-timbered, house—in some ways according to the Australian Institute of Architects, 'an uncommon example of the transitional period between Federation and the Modern Movement'.[4]

Charles was an early conservationist, even a Green.

He studied engineering in Dublin, coming to specialise in management of forests. He lost his left hand in a shooting accident when he was nineteen and learned to use a steel hook.

Before arriving in Canberra, he had drafted the *Western Australian Forests Act* in 1918, aimed at preserving native forest and to control logging, but he lost the debate. In a speech in 1920, Lane Poole said that he 'looked forward to a time when people would develop "forest conscienceness" and ensure that the forests were managed for the benefit of whole communities . . .'[5]

I suspect that at their first dinner party in Westridge discussion would've moved from trees and the great planting which was occurring throughout Canberra along the curbed and guttered and lighted streets, which were named according to theme before the building of the houses, to Ruth's work as the newly appointed first Official Advisor on Furniture to the capital.

She had just been commissioned to design the furniture and the interiors for the new Prime Minister's residence, The Lodge, and the Governor-General's residence, known now as Yarralumla or Government House.

Born in Ireland in 1885 and raised by the extended Yeats family, Ruth was trained in drawing, painting, design and embroidery at the two workshops that were a part of the Arts and Crafts movement in Dublin and which followed the ideas and practices of William Morris, the great designer and leading libertarian–socialist. Ruth would also have known of, and probably have met, some of the designers around the Omega Workshops experiment started in 1913 by Roger Fry, Vanessa Bell and Duncan Grant, and which was the production arm of the Bloomsbury Group and their ideas on aesthetics. The Bloomsbury Group was an influential bohemian elite formed just before the First World War. Several of its members had more than one sexual relationship simultaneously—sometimes heterosexual and same-sex relationships—and practised experimental parenting and educational theories. The group attracted progressive thinkers and made an impact on economic and social theory. Bloomsbury's best known members were Virginia Woolf, John Maynard Keynes, E.M. Forster, Mary (Molly) MacCarthy, Lytton Stachey, Duncan Grant, Vanessa Bell, Roger Fry, Desmond MacCarthy, Clive Bell and Leonard Woolf.

The poet William Butler Yeats gave Ruth away at her wedding to Charles in 1911, when she was twenty-six years old. Because of his appointments in Africa and other travels in the first fifteen years of their marriage they spent only five years together. They had three daughters, one named Charlotte, known as 'Charlie', who was one of the first women to get a motorbike licence in Canberra.

Now in Canberra, Ruth would've argued passionately against craftsmen being replaced by the assembly line and furniture pieces stamped out by machinery and hammered or stapled together. She would've talked in favour of simplicity, truth to materials, and unity of handicraft and design, and for traditional continuation of regional styles and practices of having self-made or artisanal created furniture and objects in the home rather than poorly made, cheap, mass-produced furnishings. She had been contributing articles on interior decoration to the *Australian Home Builder* and *Home Beautiful* magazines with headings such as 'What to do with a wall'.

Ruth Lane Poole brought with her strong ideas of how to furnish a house, how to design furniture, as the Griffins brought with them ideas of how to design a street, how to design a neighbourhood, how to make a city. As had the Griffins, she argued with the administrators, mainly over cost rather than style, but ultimately about taste. She fell afoul of the corner-cutting and fear of lavishness or 'extravagance'. But she fought.

There is a Lane Poole Place in Canberra.

At dinner with the Lane Pooles in Westridge, guests would've been stimulated to thinking that they were sitting in a grand house in a very new town intended to be the capital of a nation, having discussions with someone who had *known* Yeats and Morris and who very possibly knew some of the Bloomsbury people around the Omega Workshops.

The Lane Pooles were active in developing the social and cultural life of the national capital and I like to think that even attitudes to gastronomy were also beginning to deviate from the norm—perhaps sherry was now served as an aperitif along with Scotch, perhaps salads were tossed in the French manner, coffee and liqueurs served at the end of the meal, wine discussed before it was drunk.

The Lane Pooles organised balls to give the young cadets at the Forestry School some social life. A typical Canberra Ball was first recorded in 1925 by the *Queanbeyan Canberra Advocate.*

> *Doris Duffield's midwinter Fancy Dress fundraiser for a new organ at St John's Church was the triumph of the Hotel's first year. She and her husband (Director Mt Stromlo)* [sic] *formed the 'Stromberra' Orchestra with fellow residents Daley and Glassy, playing piano, violin, flute and bass viol and all in the costume of harlequins. Mrs Crace of Gungahlin led a party of eight Pompadours, Harriet Goodwin went*

as Bridge and Mrs Butters as Night, while the tall figure of Isabelle Southwell made a spectacular Queen of Diamonds. Cyril Davies was an unlikely Simple Simon and his wife a Chinese girl; with Mrs Rowse Persian and her husband an Arabian prince. Mrs Woodger and Della Calthorpe were Persian princesses and their auctioneer husbands convincing sheiks; Emma Rudd was artistically arranged as an Early Victorian Silhouette, while future Director of Works William Potts made a convincing Dutchman and Mr Marriott of Blandfordia was, adventurously, A Girl.[6]

There were three Marriotts listed on the 1929 electoral roll with their occupations—so this Mr Marriott, dressed as a girl, was either a clerk or a messenger. *Cold Light* has a Legacy Ball at the Hotel Canberra in the 1950s where one of my characters, Mr Thomas, a clerk at the Department of Interior, dresses as a girl.

Historian Lenore Coltheart believes that 'This splendid occasion might have been the birth of Canberra society'.[7]

In the late 1930s, the diplomatic corps began moving to Canberra when, in 1936, the United Kingdom appointed its first High Commissioner and, in 1939, when the United States established an embassy, other countries followed. The legations provided a new source of ideas and opportunities to meet people from the 'outside' world. In *Cold Light* I have my character Edith describing a social night at the Russian Minister's residence:

She'd loved the film nights at the Russian minister's home . . . She loved the pickles, the raw fish, the black bread, the caviar—oh, the caviar—and of course, the vodka, real vodka, something you couldn't

> *buy in Australia. You paid for the touch of gastronomic exotica by having to sit through Soviet films on hydro-electricity, the grain harvest, and the Moscow circus.*[8]

And then, in 1940, a couple who actually had contact with the Bloomsbury Group came to Canberra—Lyndhurst and Eilean Giblin (Lyndhurst was a Tasmanian who had gone to the United Kingdom to study and had been away from Australia for quite a while).

When the Second World War broke out, Lyndhurst left Melbourne University where he had been an economics professor and went to Canberra where he had been appointed Chairman of the Commonwealth Advisory Committee on Financial and Economic Policy.

The following descriptions of the Giblins are from the book *Giblin's Platoon*:

> *It was in these years before the First World War that Giblin sported a 'flowing Socialist beard' and declared himself a socialist virtually from birth . . . he took a 'missionary' attitude to the working class. They were to be 'raised', not rallied to. And his aspirations were far wider, more social than economic. In 1911 Giblin declared the* [Labor] *party did not need men only concerned with wages.*
>
> *In summary, Giblin was a typical 'left-liberal' of the pre-1914 world. He favoured equality, and opposed hierarchy and mere convention . . . But he was committed to the prerogative of the individual over the prerogative of the collective . . .*
>
> *He became active in Labor Party deliberations . . . He pressed for the staged nationalisation of land; voluntary voting; proportional representation; uniform divorce laws; an increased number of states . . .*[9]

At the completion of his university studies in 1917 England, Lyndhurst was introduced to the Bloomsbury Group through a friendship with a young man with Bloomsbury connections, the bisexual David 'Bunny' Garnett. There is evidence that Lyndhurst was gay or bisexual.

2.1 Two young Canberrans leaning against the collonades of the newly constructed Melbourne Building, circa 1928.

In 1918, after serving in the war, Giblin met and married Eilean Burton, in a registry office in London. She was thirty-three years old and twelve years his junior.

They shared unorthodoxy. She had distinct artistic connections and was given to 'unconventional dress' (she tended towards the masculine).

> *She was a carpenter, who made some of her own furniture . . . At the marriage ceremony there was, on her plea, no wedding ring . . . To be more exact: she would not have a ring if Lyndhurst did not have a ring. On their arrival in Hobart in 1919 Lyndhurst's mother was distressed by the ring-less finger, and Eilean relented . . .*[10]

During the Second World War, Eilean took up unpopular causes such as aid and comfort to German, Japanese and Italian POWs in concentration camps at Hay, New South Wales, which also included interned German and Italian civilians living in the United Kingdom and Australia. The Giblins had a role in organising Bertrand Russell's tour of Australia including a lecture at Canberra's Albert Hall in 1950. Russell had connections with the Bloomsbury Group.

There is a Giblin Street and a Giblin Place in Canberra and a portrait of Giblin by William Dobell hangs in the University of Melbourne.

•

In 1946, the Australian National University (ANU) was established, incorporating a university college which had been in Canberra from the thirties as a part of Melbourne University.

The main appointments to the ANU began in the 1950s, the population was about 15 000 (to rise rapidly in the 1950s to about 25 000)—and three families stand out in the 1950s for their influence on the style and nature of Canberra and their love of the dinner party.

In the 1950s, Heinz Arndt, aged thirty-six, and his wife Ruth, who had fled Hitler to study in England, came to Canberra. He had studied economics at Oxford. Ruth had studied social work at the London School of Economics. Heinz was appointed to the foundation chair of economics at the ANU. The Arndts had met at a Bloomsbury party and they'd known Lytton Strachey's nephew.

Professor Arndt was a most accomplished, respected and loved scholar, friend and Canberran. His wife Ruth was another famous Canberran (together they were a dynamic and hospitable couple known throughout Canberra). Many years later, one obituary writer wrote,

> *Heinz loved Canberra. He took pride in its growth, showing visitors its beauty of nature and design. He was an active participant in debates about the planning of Canberra throughout his life. For a period before self-government, he served as a member of the Territory's Advisory Council.*[11]

Two other appointments joined the Great Conversation—in 1950, Manning Clark was appointed to the foundation chair of history.

In 1952, he and his wife Dymphna built a house in Forrest, designed by Robin Boyd, and it is where Manning and Dymphna Clark lived and worked until their deaths. Manning Clark's roof-top study, where the six volumes of *A History of Australia* and his other works were written, dominates the design of the house and its large garden. The house is now a centre for ideas and discussion, and provides accommodation for researchers working in Canberra.

The next year, A.D. Hope, the eminent Australian poet, was appointed Professor of English, and restaurant dining had arrived in Canberra. He was known as a shy bon vivant. Hope recounts that

> . . . *in November 1968 David Campbell* [a grazier in the ACT and a well-known poet] *invited me to lunch at the Lobby Restaurant in*

Canberra where he discovered from the head waiter that they had stocks of Pokolbin wines from the recently destroyed vineyards which had been devastated by bushfires. The lunch was an epic celebration; I chiefly recall the head waiter approaching David and saying: 'Mr Campbell, it is now nearly half-past six and we are about to begin the next meal: Would you and your friend care to go on to dinner?'[12]

And they did. Campbell wrote a poem about the epic lunch/ dinner which mentions two hotel dining rooms—the Chandelier at Rydges and the Hotel Canberra, and the then new restaurant, The Lobby.

Ah Alec!
I'll be thy Herrick
When we thy guests
Meet at those lyrick Feasts,
Made at The Chandelier,
The Lobby, and Canberra, where
We such Pokolbin had
As made us nobly wise, not mad,
And yet each Verse of thine
Outdid the meats, outdid the frolick wine.[13]

Arndt, Hope, and Clark have buildings named after them at the Australian National University.

By the 1950s, the dinner table had become a suburb of Canberra—Forrest—named by the locals 'culture corner' to where academics, public servants, scientists, teachers, and people interested in the arts and public affairs had gravitated.

The conversation on *how should we shape Canberra: how should we live* continues.

Acknowledgements

Thanks go especially to Lenore Coltheart, Susan Mary Withycombe (on Eilean Giblin and other information), Tim Rowse, the three authors of *Giblin's Platoon*—William Coleman, Alf Hagger and Selwyn Cornish—Ann Gugler, Bettina Arndt, John Dargavel and Peter Freeman (on the Garden City movement and other information) and the *Australian Dictionary of Biography*.

Notes

1 Dustin Griffin, 2008.*The Writings of Walter Burley Griffin*, Cambridge University Press, New York. p. 274.
2 Antoine Faivre, 1987. 'Theosophy', in Mircea Eliade, Charles J. Adams, et al. *The Encyclopedia of Religion*, Macmillan, New York.
3 Jill Roe, 2010. 'Marion, Miles, and the Magic of America'. Marion Mahony Griffin Lecture 21 April 2010, National Library of Australia Theatre, Canberra.
4 Australian Institute of Architects, *Register of Significant Twentieth Century Architecture* (RSTCA) report RO19, 1984.
5 Quoted in Michael Calver, Heidi Bigler-Cole, Geoffrey Bolton, Andrea Gaynor, Pierre Horwitz, Jenny Mills, Grant Wardell-Johnson, 2005. *A Forest Conscienceness: Proceedings 6th National Conference of the Australian Forest History Society Inc.* Millpress Science Publishers, Rotterdam.
6 Available online at <http://nla.gov.au/nla.news-title119>.
7 Lenore Coltheart, personal conversation with author.
8 Frank Moorhouse, 2011. *Cold Light*, Random House, Sydney, p. 281.
9 W. Coleman, A. Hagger, S. Cornish, 2006. *Giblin's Platoon: The trials and triumph of the economist in Australian public life*, ANU Press, Canberra.
10 *ibid.*

11 Ross Garnaut and Hal Hill, *ANU Reporter*, 24 May 2002.
12 A.D. Hope 1978. *A Book of Answers*, Angus and Robertson, Sydney.
13 Written 7 November 1968, Quoted in A.D. Hope, *ibid.*

3

A CITY OF THE MIND

Marion Halligan

Canberra is a city that existed in sophisticated detail in its designers' imaginations long before any building was done. It has always been a city of the mind and, ever since it was no more than a figment of the imagination, all sorts of people have claimed to be heirs of its vision. I am interested in writing about a city which has this intense phantasmagoric life in the minds of all sorts of people who thus in a sense own it, and consider they know what is best for it. In fact they are creating their own city in their own image. This is one of the things I am talking about in the opening pages of my novel *The Point*. I invented a restaurant, on the lake between the National Library and the National Gallery of Australia, about where there is a glamorous eating house now, but mine is on a small promontory of land, an almost-island. The first word of the novel is *Imagine*: 'Imagine—or you could try going and looking, if the place and the time were right, if the light fell in a certain way and you had eyes to see—otherwise, imagine . . . It is unlikely that all those propitious requirements will be met, but in the world of the imagination, not impossible.'

Since I was inventing this restaurant I decided to have it designed by Marion Mahony Griffin. None of the buildings in Canberra are in fact hers, but she did fill the plans with wonderful drawings which give us an idea of the sort of thing that might have been built. Very feminine buildings, with lots of glass, with breast-shaped cupolas, all reflected in limpid pools. I made my restaurant an octagon, with seven of its walls made of glass. It is like a lantern. The people outside can see in, but the people inside cannot see out. Inside are those who possess, who possibly are possessed, outside are the dispossessed. Who can see what they do not have.

When the book was finished, but before it was published, I went to an exhibition at the National Archives of Marion Mahony's drawings for Canberra. They are done with fine drawn lines on gold silk, and are very fragile. They cannot be brightly lit. And there I found my restaurant, exactly as I had described it. Except hers was on the other side of the lake, by Mount Ainslie. The octagonal shape, the glass walls, the dome, like a lantern, and its dotted outline reflected in water. I am sure I had never seen the drawing before.

•

In the life of the imagination, it is surprising how often such serendipitous things happen.

A friend of mine went to London in the late 1950s, when she was not quite twenty. She explored the city on foot, taking with her the *Baedeker* guide her father had used on his trip to London when he was much the same age, in the 1930s. A lot of the buildings were no longer there. She walked around streets, gap-toothed where buildings had been bombed out of existence, sometimes the

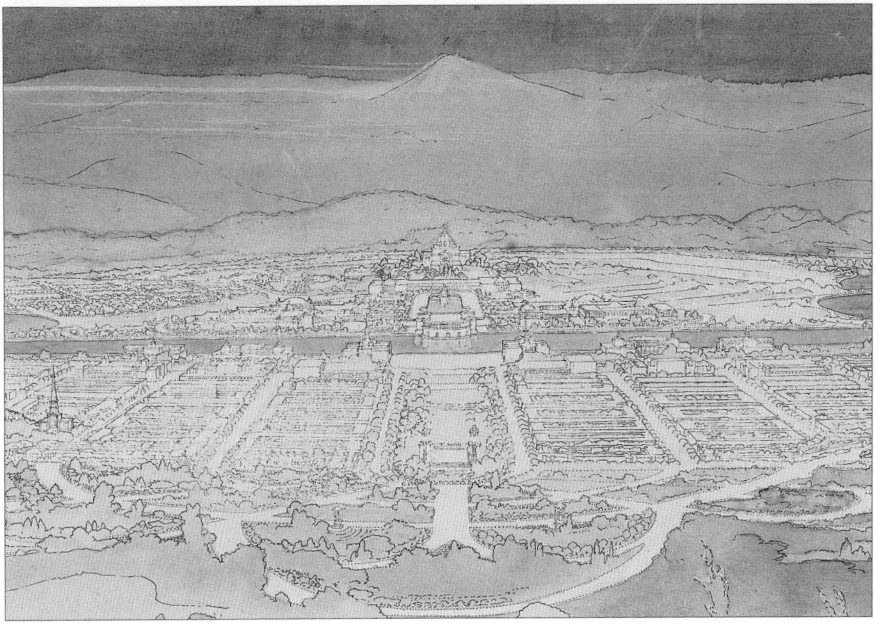

3.1 'View from the summit of Mount Ainslie' by Marion Mahony Griffin.

remnants in heaps of rubble, sometimes cleared away, sometimes replaced by new edifices.

She found this exciting. It was profoundly melancholy, and yet in a curious way those buildings, still in *Baedeker* but no longer in London, had a powerful presence in her mind and, to this day, her London is a place of buildings and of the phantoms of buildings. She hadn't thought when she took with her that pre-war *Baedeker*, how much would have changed. This pilgrimage, you could call it, through the city that once was, as well as the city of the aftermath of the blitz, was a gift she is still grateful for.

I have in my mind a kind of Ur-Sydney, from the same period, when we would take the train the hundred miles south from Newcastle to the glorious metropolis and wander about it, to theatres and galleries and shops. We stayed at the YWCA, that bastion of female virtue, with its vast marble reception desk keeping all males out. Rowe Street was still there, with its little art shops; the great demolitions had hardly begun. Sydney was still largely Victorian and Art Deco, its masses not so much tall as broad and heavily decorated. I think I still believe in this Sydney.

•

Canberra, unlike most cities in the world, existed fairly whole in the minds of the people who could be said to have invented it. The whole that we live in is of course quite a lot different from their conceptions and, to a certain extent, that was probably inevitable, but perhaps not so drastically. Mostly we refused to be faithful to their vision, and continue to do so. Though various bodies make claims to be the heirs of Griffin and his legacy, both have been treated cavalierly.

I have lived in the city now for nearly fifty years; in fact, on the occasion of its centenary, I will have lived here for more than half its life. More than a decade before I came to Canberra I had pictures of it in my head. When I was a child the woman who lived up the street in a pretty Edwardian villa, even closer to the sea than we were, used to have visits from her granddaughter, who lived in Canberra. The girl was a bit older than me, but we liked to play together. She enjoyed a pedagogical relationship with me and was always telling me things. So I knew from her that Canberra was considered to be a difficult place to live, a hardship posting, she called it, so people got extra money for putting up with it. Everybody had a hedge, the plants given by the government, and a man came regularly and cut it. She was obviously something of a parrot, this girl, repeating what she heard grown-ups say, but also quite a storyteller, for I had in my mind a mythical, mysterious place, not at all like the blustery seaside city where I lived. And when she described the hardship posting it was evident that it was also a great privilege.

This is still true, the hardship and the privilege. The rest of the country has its own view of Canberra, and frequently a pejorative one. The other day, in the car, I was listening to a program about self-rule for the Northern Territory. People kept saying that it was ruled from Canberra, and it was quite inappropriate, they said, that the Northern Territory should be ruled from Canberra; such a large and individual place should have its own government, not be ruled from Canberra. After some time of this I was shouting back at the radio: What do you mean, you total idiots? Ruled from Canberra? We're not allowed to rule even ourselves let alone anywhere else. What you are trying to say in your numbskulled way is that it is ruled by the federal government. This is typical of the big bad bossy Canberra throwing its weight around—an image that so many people have of the place. The wicked bogeyman. I remember being in Melbourne in the days of Malcolm Fraser's razor gangs in the late 1970s and realising it wasn't politic to say you came from Canberra; shopkeepers could get quite nasty and serve you rudely. If you parked your car in certain places, you ran the risk of people taking their keys and scratching long lines in the duco.

But when I came as a university student to live in Bruce Hall I had no idea of this, I just knew about the hedges and the hardship. And the fact that it was cold. Every time somebody congratulated me on my luck in coming here they said, oh, but it's cold, you'll be so cold. This in fact was quite wrong. I have never in Canberra been so cold as I was at home in Newcastle in that draughty little wooden seaside house, with a small patent grate in which a coal fire was lit in the evenings, never any heat in the mornings, or during the day. We went to bed in flannel nightgowns and layers of blankets, with our feet in the sleeves of a woollen cardigan that we wrapped around them. People still say, Canberra: it's cold isn't it. In Bruce Hall I had to sleep with the window open a little, otherwise you got boiled alive by the central heating. Now that I mostly stay home all day, I sit in my warm study and look at the sunny world outside and think what a happy climate I live in.

Of course, coldness was a factor in the minds of the founding fathers. They believed that human beings' brains worked better in a cold climate, so they thought our rulers would do a better job of thinking how to govern us. No tropical indolence. I don't suppose they imagined us all sitting toastily in centrally heated rooms.

•

Sometimes people who read my novels express interest in the Canberra they find there. This is usually a matter of particular enjoyment as they did not know it was a city like that: mainly a city like any other, with poor people and people struggling, getting involved in little crimes and generally finding life hard. Sometimes sleeping with their children in cars or under bridges. It is a difficult city to be poor in because of the cold; that toasty central heating costs a great deal of money. So does an inefficient little electric radiator.

The bushfires had a similar effect: the rest of the country seemed surprised to find that Canberra was subject to the same inexorable natural forces as the rest of the country. Just fancy, our houses burn down too. My novel *The Apricot Colonel* begins with the bushfires and ends with Australia entering the Iraq war, after the great march that formed a tail-in-mouth serpent all around Civic, to no avail. My readers were interested in the unexpected Canberra they found in those pages.

Several of the characters in *The Point* are homeless people who live on the hot-air vents of the National Library. I'd been in Paris walking along streets and realised how warm the air was that came pouring out of gratings against the pavement, and how cosy it was for the people sleeping there. (The air was not fresh, rather stale in fact, but it was hot.) They had beds set up with sheets of cardboard and coverings; one man had his clock on the low sill of a window. People tucked up early. Soon after I was walking on the grass outside the National Library, and noticed the building had hot-air vents at ground level. So I imagined people sleeping there, as they would in Paris. As far as I know nobody actually does this, but were they to begin doing so it would be a rather nice example of life imitating art. Fiction can make such things happen, especially when they are so logical as this.

Responses to *The Point* were fascinating to me. The lake is a character in it. Clovis the homeless man spends a lot of time looking at it, thinking about it, finding words for all its various manifestations. As locals know, it is not a blue lake, almost never; it is silver and pewter and grey, often luminous, or sparkling, but not blue. People said to me, after reading this novel, that they started to look at the lake. They said, I drive round it, or over it, every day, I ride my bicycle along it, I walk from bridge to bridge, but I have never thought of really looking at it before. It gave them great pleasure to have their perceptions widened in this way. I think that this is one of the things novels do, allow us to see our world in new ways. Written down.

•

The lake. I am an ante-diluvian resident; I lived here before it was made. When I was in Bruce Hall a friend was invited to a concert at the Albert Hall by a careful young man. I thought we could walk, he said. Won't it be muddy? she asked. I have brought paper tissues, he said. It was a long way, over to University House then along where the National Museum of Australia is now, the hospital then, over Lennox Crossing which later I would drive across to teach at Canberra High, now the art school. Lennox Crossing was one of those low bridges, really just the road slightly raised above the lake bed. It was lined with the most glorious poplars. And yes, it was muddy. She never went out with him again.

When I came to live in Bruce Hall at the beginning of 1962, it had Oxbridge aspirations: gowns to be worn to formal meals, Latin grace spoken, high table convened. Coffee or tea elegant in the Junior Common Room after dinner. These came out of urns we reckoned were interchangeable and not properly washed; the coffee tasted of tea, the tea of coffee. Neither attractive. That first night we were sitting in a group of new people being informed by an old hand, a young man with hair in a shock, buck teeth, thick glasses, ancient flannels and Harris tweed sports coat. The place to go for coffee was the Blue Moon Café, he said. And we didn't need any money; the wonderful thing was, everybody took cheques, it really was a cashless society.

So off we all trotted, down to the Blue Moon Café in Garema Place. In those days University Avenue ran straight from Civic to the front of Bruce Hall, then did a right turn and went off up to the wilds of Belconnen. Lying in bed at night you could hear the trucks changing gear as they rounded the bend. We had our coffee, the young man offered a cheque (I have a feeling it was about six shillings), the café refused it, he had no cash, so we all dug out enough to pay for it. I got to know that road to town, it was really the only way to get there; I don't remember a bus.

3.2 Monaro Mall in 1963 was Australia's first three-level covered shopping mall.

The Blue Moon stayed for quite a long time, for a good bit of its life a smart continental delicatessen. There was another café, Lumby's, downstairs in Bailey Arcade; you went there for coffee and cake after the movies. And there was the Pendulum, also in Garema Place, which had good jazz.

If you wanted continental movies you went to Queanbeyan, as you did for salami. Because Italians lived there.

If you wanted to dance you went to the Canberra Rex, at the end of the week. There were bands, and at ten o'clock supper was brought out, usually chicken à la King, free, so that people could continue to drink as well as dance. The liquor licence didn't allow for drinking without food. At midnight the band played 'When the Saints Go Marching In', and everybody went home. In those days I had a fondness for Brandy Alexanders. Evidence that the past is another country, and I am a different person. The Rex had a fine dining room, with a very grand *maitre d'hôtel*, a portly gentleman who later turned up as a sort of floorwalker at David Jones.

•

Living in Bruce Hall was luxury, looking back on it. The rooms cleaned every week day, all meals provided. I think we knew how good it was, but we couldn't wait to get out of it and keep house for ourselves. We wanted to be our own people, not wear gowns to meals and, if we were late, stand behind our chairs until the warden nodded for us to sit down. We believed it was malice when he failed to notice us for quite a long time, pouring the wine at high table. After spending a lot of time searching, a colleague and I found what called itself a flat: a double garage with a small room on one side that served as a laundry for upstairs and a kitchen for us, and a couple of bedrooms. It was in Red Hill, with a view across the city. It was the house of a builder, who had the not uncommon habit of constructing the garage and living in it with his wife and numerous children while he finished the house above, an early kind of McMansion. He showed signs while we were there of starting the whole process again, but his wife was fed up. She had a house at last and wanted to keep it.

The same year I met my future husband who had come to Canberra for a job, and six months later we got married. This was a mistake; if he'd been married before he came, the university would have given us a house at a highly subsidised rent, which we could have bought. Even if we'd been engaged, this would have happened. Trouble was, we didn't meet until after he came, so no luck.

He was offered a bed-sitting room in a block of flats in O'Connor, not yet built. He went to see the government housing officer, a Mr Bird, who was sympathetic: yes, that was no good for a married couple; he'd put us down for a one-bedroom flat. In the meantime we lived in the double garage, where I had come down with pneumonia three weeks before the wedding.

Before the year was out, Mr Bird, known as Dickie, was in trouble with the law for fiddling housing lists in return for bribes, and the whole business of our flat fell through. He never mentioned his consideration towards us, so perhaps some clients he helped out of kindness. Our only solution was to buy a house as, it turned out, a mortgage was cheaper than rents made exorbitant by so much subsidising.

But where? It had to be a new suburb because of the government loan. (Thirty-four years later, when my husband died, I paid this out. In all that period of small deposits we had repaid almost none of the capital, only the very low interest.) Canberra has always had a habit of opening up new suburbs sequentially. Hackett was nearly full. Hughes was beginning, but we had more sense than to go there; Hackett was disappointingly distant but Hughes was the end of the earth. So we bought in Hackett, not the Heights which cost extra, but lower down, in what my husband liked to call Hackett Downs, and was mostly disappointed when no one thought it funny. I mentioned it recently, as a joke, to a real estate agent who did me a property profile, even though I promised him I had no intention of selling. He wrote, 'Tranquil, space & light—this fabulous north facing home snookered away in central Hackett Downs . . .' Snookered: there's a good verb.

I like to look at the photos of those days. The front yard a stretch of churned-up mud, not a tree in sight, not even the ubiquitous planted street trees (gorgeous tall liquidambars). The tallest vegetation was a stalk of paspalum. Mount Ainslie was very close to the back yard; Mount Majura just at the end of the curve of the front street. Now you can almost never see either; I have done my bit for the urban forest of Canberra. Not least in four mighty oaks, all that remains of the dozens that grew from the children's picking up tiny acorns and dropping them on the ground.

Canberra made gardeners of us. In my day you got forty shrubs and ten trees when you bought a new house. Some of these remain. I had to have my dead silver birch chopped down recently. The tree man kept telling me how dangerous it was, totally rotten. It was a very beautiful tree in its time, and I was sorry to see it go. The mulberry was a disappointment: the fruit lacks sugar and acid and is tasteless; even children aren't much interested in it. I made jam, not nice, so we tried turning the berries into wine. We had to add extra sugar and lemon juice, and needed to add a yeast to make it start fermenting. It ended up at eighteen per cent alcohol, and tasted vile. I imagine you could have got a stunning hangover from it. The birds, however, have a good time: the noisy friar birds get drunk on the berries and sometimes fly into the windows; they lie about for a bit then fly away.

Most of the other trees and shrubs we bought at nurseries. That free issue (these days you get a certain amount of money to spend) converted us. Now and then you see a house that never took up its allowance, how sad it looks, among its embowered neighbours. I grew up in Newcastle by the sea. So I longed for trees, which didn't grow in the salty climate, and roses. The typical garden was a square of buffalo grass with concrete-edged flowerbeds along the house walls, with portulaca, geraniums, stocks sometimes, marigolds, petunias, colourful things, annuals mostly. When I was eighteen I went to a nursery and bought trees that would flourish in the sea air, and they did, wonderfully: pohutekawa and something called Norfolk Island Christmas bush. They were still going strong when the house was moved up to a dairy farm in the Hunter Valley (so I heard) and an Art Deco-ish oceanliner-style mansion built in its place, with a view I suppose of the sea. I wonder if those trees are still there.

•

I did not imagine I would be still living in Canberra, after all these years. I meant to stay for a year, two at most. So did my husband. He did get other jobs, including in his native country of New Zealand, but somehow we didn't want to go when it came to the point. The children were horrified that we could even think of it. When he died I could have gone back, but didn't want to, not so many decades on.

I always imagined I would not be able to live away from the sea, having grown up beside it, but somehow I do. I go and stay at Noah's on its promontory between Newcastle Beach and the harbour, and think I will come and live here, but since I can't really afford even a night there that is unlikely to happen.

I do, however, have a theory that the reason the rest of the country misprizes Canberrans is this sense that we are up ourselves, here in the high country. The sea shore, even many miles away as it is for so many Sydneysiders, is the place to be.

But I have fallen in love with the light of Canberra, its clarity and distance, its hills that turn pink at the day's end. Of course people do love the places where they live, even the unprepossessing ones, and Canberra is hardly that. What if, we say, and I being a writer say it more than most. What if . . . we had gone to New Zealand, back to Newcastle, down to Melbourne. We would have missed an adventure.

•

I sometimes wonder whether having existed is a good enough reason for being remembered? Is it nostalgia of an idle kind, or perhaps sentimentality, which we have made a rude word? But of course I don't think that. We all live in a past, a present, and a future. Some of us pay attention only to the present and the future. Some, quite dangerously I believe, look only to the future, and spend all their time dwelling on what (they expect) will come, not paying attention to what is being and what has been. I am old enough to have suffered many losses, and sometimes I want to remember the past as though I am still living it, as indeed it is still alive in my contemplation of it.

This city of the mind is part of my past in the present, too.

4

AN IDEAL CITY

David Headon

The tired old jokes about Canberra have been knocking about for decades. 'The ruin of a good sheep station,' according to quite a few rural Australians over the years. 'A bunch of suburbs in search of a city', the nation's urban dwellers have crowed. Perhaps most insistent of all, the wry comment probably first voiced in the 1950s, the national capital dismissed as nothing better than a cemetery . . . with lights.

Throughout the last century, as the Canberra region grew from a clump of isolated sheep stations in the early Federation years into a capital city in the new millennium of well over 300 000, ridicule in the media continued unchecked. Tabloid editorial writers and radio 'shock jocks' of the past, caught short for copy, often resorted to Canberra-bashing as an easy fix on a slow day, establishing a long-term pattern of nationwide response not easily dismissed or dismantled. Throw into the mix the certainty that some federal politicians of any era will always act in a manner unbecoming, a manner that inevitably prompts the knee-jerk response that Canberra is 'on the nose', and you have the lazy narrative of last resort.

On 12 March 2013, Australia's capital city celebrated its one-hundredth year, an anniversary rightly generating an abundance of community celebration and excitement. Yet it is also a symbolic marker in the city's history demanding something more, a retrospect commensurate with this milestone significance. For Canberra has a fascinating foundation story to tell, one entirely at odds with the worn clichés, a story of a city in fact built on ambition, determination, creativity and vision. It is a compelling narrative, and it needs a centenary airing. Canberra's story is an integral part, in certain ways an inspiring part, of Australia's story.

In the first half of the twentieth century, Australia, like so many countries across the globe, was force-fed with economic depression and world wars. The preceding fifty years, however, the second half of the nineteenth century, was conspicuous for a sense of community aspiration and activity that would not be contained. Fortunes were made, on the land, on the sheep's back, in rich gold mines and through an eager take-up of new technologies, creating an Australian middle class by 1901 that was, according to respected Australian economic historians, as affluent as any in the world. The cluster of international trade and cultural expositions that began with Joseph Paxton's Crystal Palace in London in 1851 and continued apace to St. Louis and Paris in 1900 (some sixteen genuine international expos in fifty years) included no less than four in the Australian colonies. Sydney (1879), Melbourne (1880, 1888) and Adelaide (1887) all assumed hosting duties. Many Australian colonists of the era either took to travelling the world, or attracted the best the world had to offer right into their own back yard.

In this climate of discovery, flair and innovation, and with a brand new century beckoning, Australian thoughts turned to the prospect of creating a nation out of a few rival colonies. Nineteenth-century poet, James Brunton Stephens, in the same 1870s decade that witnessed the first combative pro-Australian sentiments across the colonies, penned his heavily anthologised poem, 'The Dominion of Australia (A Forecast)'. It begins:

She is not yet; but he whose ear
Thrills to that finer atmosphere
Where footfalls of appointed things,
Reverberant of days to be,
Are heard in forecast echoings,
Like wave-beats from a viewless sea—
Hears in the voiceful tremors of the sky
Auroral heralds whispering, 'She is nigh'.[1]

Stephens looked to a time, soon, when 'all our land, Australia Felix called, / Become one Continent-Isle of Emerald'. While he tugged unashamedly at the heart-strings, in the last part of the century a growing number of hard-nosed professional pundits began to voice the economic and political sense of the Federation argument. And, besides, it was high time that Australasian XIs, when beating the Poms at cricket, walked onto the green swaths of the SCG and MCG as Australian XIs.

The Federation discussion, when it began in earnest at the beginning of the 1890s, was vigorous and sophisticated. All six of the colonies at that time enjoyed a form of self-government, five of them for the best part of forty years. Henry Parkes, in his eighties, though as ego-driven as ever and determined to be remembered as the 'Father of Federation' (which he wasn't), supplied the elevated phrasing at the 1890 Australasian Federation Conference, in Melbourne, when he spoke of the 'crimson thread of kinship [that] runs through us all'.[2] But it was left to an impressive list of much younger participants, including Alfred Deakin, Samuel Griffith, Andrew Inglis Clark and William McMillan to conjure a mood which shortly after resulted in the National Australasian Convention, held in Sydney in March/April 1891. This convention was specifically tasked with exploring the detail of an Australian Federation.

Each colony sent a delegation, and an agreement was reached on the formation of three committees: one to investigate the finance of tax and trade; another to consider a federal judiciary; and, most importantly, a third to draft a constitution bill to establish a Commonwealth of States. In the midst of the constitution bill plenary debate, respected South Australian representative Richard Chaffey Baker suggested that while the 'burning question' of the prospective new nation's capital city would in time have to be discussed at length, he advocated 'the postponement of its settlement to a more convenient season'.[3] Even at this preliminary stage, the key players—among them Alfred Deakin, Samuel Griffith, Edmund Barton, Charles Kingston and John Downer (a veritable who's who of Canberra city's elegant inner suburbs!)—recognised that the complex capital discussion had to be as informed as possible. They were only too aware of its potential to be both controversial and divisive. Not a burning question so much as a ticking bomb.

Yet it soon became clear that while the colonial delegates, mostly lawyers, might opt for pragmatic postponement of the issue, rank-and-file Australians were having none of that. Indeed, as the 1890s progressed, and Federation's fortunes waxed and waned and waxed

4.1 Edward Thomas Luke photograph in 'Tour of Senators' album: Senators on peak of Mount Conobolas, Orange. This site was a prominent national capital option in early 'Battle of the Sites' years, 1902–3.

again, one constant remained. The proud citizens of cities, towns and hamlets across the country insisted on having their say on the capital question. Customs duties and High Court protocols held limited popular interest. The site and character of the capital city, however, was altogether different. On this matter, they demanded a say.

The cocky residents of the two urban powerhouses, Sydney and Melbourne, anticipated a race in two. Surely the capital could only be hosted, they felt, either by 'Marvellous Melbourne' or the pride of New South Wales, its shimmering harbour city? They couldn't have been more wrong. The queue of alternative contenders, Australia-wide, formed in a hurry, ranging from the zealous utopian visions and the odd carefully reasoned plan of highly motivated individual citizens to the propaganda promotions of whole communities.

In 1894, Sydney surveyor and engineer F. Oliver Jones named his imagined imperial capital, 'Pacivica', a resplendent 'City Beautiful' in the virgin bush of Kuringai Chase on the banks of the Hawkesbury River. In Pacivica, character-building and nation-building sport would create a cleansed race of Empire Britons adhering to the strictures of muscular Christianity. In the same year, radical Queensland journalist and politician J.G. Drake wrote an article for the 'Bushman's Bible', the *Bulletin,* locating his model at Cameron Corner, where the arid inland borders of New South Wales, Queensland and South Australia meet. Consistent with the race-driven community values of the time, Drake imagined a white warrior race cheerfully procreating to populate nearby towns such as Cunnamulla, Charleville, Thargomindah and Bourke. No blacks allowed, or even contemplated. The Drake model was so seriously promoted that, in 1896, it was published as a booklet in Brisbane under the title, *Federation, Imperial or Democratic.* Another *Bulletin* writer in 1896 opted for a similar community, but located in what he depicted as the purifying isolation of South Australia's MacDonnell ranges.[4]

While extreme bush options had a certain appeal as Russel Ward's 'Australian Legend' cultural forces of white egalitarianism gathered strength, most of the proposals in the 1890s decade were of a more grounded kind, based on perceived regional advantage. Echuca, Corowa and Albury, for example, boasted about their location in the Murray River corridor. Ballarat and Bendigo pointed to the evidence that their abundant fields of gold had produced an urban architectural splendour and amenity that could be readily adapted to federal use. Mount Gambier extolled the virtues of its mild climate, fine scenery and perceived prime strategic location, while Port Augusta optimistically pitched itself as a hub for inter-colonial and international ocean trade.

Fired up by the sudden Federation buzz across the continent in 1890, one South Australian Legislative Councillor, Dr Allan Campbell, addressing the citizens of Port Augusta in a talk entitled 'Federation and South Australia', could barely contain himself as he concluded with a rhetorical flourish obviously wooing local votes: 'Where then can a situation be selected for the future seat of Federal Government possessing such advantages as Port Augusta offers? I do not see one on the whole map!'[5] It's not clear precisely what map Councillor Campbell was using at the time, but it certainly elicited a forthright claim—one contested as a matter of course, with similar parochialism, right across the country for the best part of a decade. All comers fancied their chances.

The Australian Constitution, when ratified at the beginning of a new century, changed the game entirely. Amid intense political lobbying (and a telling threat by New South Wales Premier George Reid that if his colony did not host the capital, it wanted no part of Federation), Section 125 confirmed that the site would be in New South Wales. The other colonies, however, were equally adamant that it would not be Sydney, lest the Mother Colony's premier city dominate them forever more. The city must be at least one hundred miles from Sydney and, until the site was selected, Melbourne would play host. Victorians sensed an opportunity to make the temporary permanent.

And so began a new and industrious second phase in the capital saga, as the issue became more urgent. With the notion of a 'bush capital' in effect legislated for, fresh questions arose, and plenty of them. What region of New South Wales was most suitable? Would the new capital be constructed from the ground up? How big should the federal territory enfolding the city be? Would this fledgling city of the New World be based on the cities of the Old World? On established design principles of the Old World? Or should Australia's new city strike out for its own uncharted design terrain? Siting, clearly, was now only one of a myriad number of strategic and cultural considerations.

Between Federation and the beginning of the Great War, 1901 to 1914, the sporadic outbreaks of capital activity variously involved the politicians, the design professionals, the people at large, purposeful foreigners and combinations of all four. The reasons are simply put: the politicians knew that they had to get involved because Section 125 was not going away. Some willingly grasped the challenge, just as others eschewed a question that at the end of the day did not interest them. The design professionals found intoxicating the stimulus of a new capital city for a new nation. Their passion and professional interest surfaced immediately. Community interest never really wavered. Vested interests abounded, yes, but all tended to be modified and ultimately re-shaped by an overarching commitment to excellence, to the creation of a capital that would be a resounding global advertisement set to interest and attract overseas talent. The new democratic kid on the southern-hemisphere block was determined to make firm all its foundations.

Those politicians in the inaugural Commonwealth parliament (meeting for the first time in Melbourne on 9 May 1901) who might have regarded the capital issue as their sole preserve, had no time to impose their opinions. For coinciding exactly with parliament's historic first session, just down Collins Street no more than a hundred metres away from the deliberating politicians, the design professionals held their own milestone gathering, the 'Congress of Engineers, Architects, Surveyors and Others Interested in the Building of the Federal Capital of Australia, 1901'. The Congress, which ran from 6 May to 17 May, one of the first of its kind in the English-speaking world, passed two significant resolutions. The first stated that an 'independent' report compiled by the design professions must precede any capital-city site decision by government; the second, reflecting a tangible engagement with the most progressive design ideas from overseas, advocated the laying out of the Federal Capital 'in the most perfect manner possible'. Delegates refused to countenance any 'obstructions . . . that would in any way prevent the adoption of the most perfect design'.[6] Near enough was simply not good enough.

From the time Daniel Burnham gathered together a cohort of America's most talented architects to construct the renowned 'White City' for the World's Columbian Exposition in Chicago in 1893, the idea of the 'City Beautiful' had captured everyone's imagination. This was obvious in Melbourne, eight years later, when engineer George Higgins delivered the inaugural address to his Congress colleagues. Higgins dwelt on the unprecedented opportunity—a once-in-a-lifetime chance—for his generation of Australian professionals to build 'a model city', an 'ideal city'. His stirring words set the tone for all the papers that followed, most of which aspired to a standard for the Australian capital that today would be labelled 'world's best practice'.[7] Integral questions surrounding water access, sewerage disposal, traffic flow and business regulations were canvassed, but the two papers in the *Proceedings* of the Congress that catch the eye of a present-day reader were those delivered by George Sydney Jones and the Director of the Royal Horticultural Gardens in Burnley (Melbourne), Charles Bogue Luffmann. Both men addressed the Congress brief with due diligence, while reaching for something beyond, the key symbolic issues transcending practical considerations.

Jones articulated the *character* of the capital he had in mind, a city with its own genuinely independent identity, in a telling passage that linked seamlessly to the prevailing Australian Federation zeitgeist:

> *Firstly, then, as to the spirit which should characterize the architecture of the City. What should it be? Surely it should be the common-sense 20th Century spirit of the Australian, that owns no style . . . that can produce simple and true construction, that can produce dignity and truth of exterior from excellence of plan, and above all that can produce that refined thoughtfulness of design which is so conspicuous in the best work of our time and race . . . Let us, for heaven's and the people's sake, not slavishly copy the art of past dead centuries, even though it be the purity and grace of the Greek, or the mystery and impressiveness of the art of the middle ages, or the magnificence and display of the great age of the Renaissance. With thought and care and study (of which there seems but little in some directions now-a-days) it is possible to create Architecture which is purely Australian, which, while possessing the best*

> *of the characteristics of the above-mentioned great ages of art, shall reflect also the best, in thought and spirit, which in so comparatively short a time has made us what we are.*[8]

This was a statement as incisive in its projection of contemporary Australia at the time of Federation as it was impatient for a liberated future.

Not to be outdone, and sticking closely to his own field of expertise, Bogue Luffmann also endeavoured to break free of the remnant colonial shackles. He proposed an 'agricultural, horticultural and sylvan' bush capital, recommending seven specific features of his city of the future that included a 'true botanic garden, representing Australia[n] flora'. Many decades in advance of the Australian gardener's zealous affection for native flora, Luffmann's combative horticultural philosophy closely aligned with George Jones' broader cultural map. The Commonwealth's new capital city had to be environmentally attuned to, and reflective of, the spirit of Federation:

> *Let us beware of introducing an exotic plan or arrangement of scenes. To look out on bits of Italy, or Norway, or Japan, will be defects indeed. No imitations of Tivoli, Versailles, Aranguez [sic], Interlaken, or Granada will be appropriate. Nor even a Derby dale, Devonshire lane, or English royal or family park should be figured here. If we must have symbols, let us typify our own . . . our heritage must be kept in sight, our Gippsland stream and valley, our Blue Mountain escarpment, timbered crag, wind-swept cataract and highland plateau, for waratah, rock lily, callistemon, kurrajong, banksia, wattle, and flannel flower, in their place and season. Let us have reminders of the Hawkesbury*

> *and the Macquarie, in richly wooded cone and clear silent lake, or jungle-crowned morass, and examples of our warm New England hills and more distant northern downs. Our South and West Australian billabong and pine ridge, with mulga, epacris and spinifex where each will thrive, must be represented, and our bracing Tasmanian range with its attendant reach of water and vegetation. There is no reason why all the most typical and worthy features of the Federated States may not be embodied in the scenery, for the climate of the hill country of Southern New South Wales favours the most diverse vegetation.*[9]

Bogue Luffmann understood that the foundations for an independent capital city started with the enlightened mindset of its citizens.

It is possible to suggest, with the benefit of hindsight, that the 1901 Melbourne Congress set the tone of what followed in the years leading up to the Great War, as politicians, professionals and hobby planners all contributed to the quality of the capital city discussion—and, with it, to a steady increase in momentum. In the national parliament, this started with a provocative motion moved on 19 July 1901 in the House of Representatives that 'in the interest of human progress' the government must secure for the nation's capital '1,000 square miles of land in a good, healthy and fertile situation'. The mover of this motion was an American (who had to say he was Canadian-born in order to stand for election in Australia), the extroverted, eccentric, 'legendary' King O'Malley.[10]

What a story. He was an incorrigible teller of tall tales about himself, but he didn't need to be. The truth does well enough. In the decade or so ahead, the same O'Malley would become the Commonwealth's Minister for Home Affairs in Andrew Fisher's second Labor government

4.2 Historic Claude Vautin photograph captures the moment as King O'Malley, the Commonwealth Minister for Home Affairs, hammers in the first peg to symbolically begin the city of Canberra's survey on Camp Hill, part of Kurrajong (now Capital) Hill, 20 February 1913.

(the Party's third) during the seminal years, 1910–13. He would be responsible for introducing the first Ordinance of the Federal Capital Territory, in January 1911—prohibition—which would stay on the books for the next seventeen years; responsible for the transcontinental railway; arguably responsible for the founding of the Commonwealth Bank; and totally responsible for Canberra's most important first national day, 12 March 1913, when the foundation stones were laid and the city formally named.

The last living member of the first national parliament when he died in 1953, O'Malley grabbed the attention of his colleagues with his far-sighted 1901 motion, not only advocating that the Australian people in principle should 'own' the land of the federal territory, but challenging his parliamentary colleagues to conduct any future capital discussion in a manner befitting its high national significance:

> *The great Commonwealth has now before it a supreme specified duty to perform in the erection of the federal capital upon ground held in fee-simple of the nation; property that shall belong to the whole people, and not to a few comatose monopolists. The federal capital, or the home of the people of the Commonwealth should be built in harmony with the artistic spirit of progressive civilisation . . . We must remember that in this matter we are not acting for ourselves alone, but for countless millions of unbegotten generations of future ages.*[11]

Of course, a harmonious and artistic capital, constructed in the 'virgin' bush from the ground up, must have a salubrious site that would make the dream possible.

So began the 'tours' of the Senators and House members, throughout New South Wales, to identify the most suitable region for a model city of the future. From the outset, two things were unofficially understood by the many parliamentarians who took an active interest: one, a coastal town was a most unlikely choice because of the fear of disease spreading at sea-level heat as plague, and the possibility of enemy bombardment from the sea; and two, the corollary, an inland capital city in a cooler region had the most appeal because, in addition to not having sea level's disadvantages, there was the almost universal belief at the time that people of European descent were best equipped to assume their (perceived) rightful place at the forefront of human civilisation if they were raised in chilly climes. This 'cold climate myth', absurd to us now, was expressed with typical literary audacity by King O'Malley in an 8 October 1903 House debate when he proclaimed that 'The history of the world shows that cold climates have produced the greatest geniuses, all of whom were born north of a certain degree'.[12] Given the inherent problem that remote Australia was a hemisphere south of that degree, the Federation fathers had to settle for south of Goulburn.

Despite what from a distance looks like a gentlemen's agreement on the selection criteria, the 'Battle of the Sites' still took six years (1902–08) to settle and, as Gavin Souter points out in *Acts of Parliament* (1988), involved no less than seven Commonwealth governments, five New South Wales governments, two Royal Commissions, nine Commonwealth Ministers for Home Affairs, four lapsed Bills and three Acts of the Commonwealth Parliament. One of the latter was a *Seat of Government Act 1904* that gave the capital to the remote southern town of Dalgety, a full four years before Canberra got the nod.

This 'battle' was not easily won, and before Canberra was finally endorsed in December 1908, all of the prominent Federation founders had declared their position, often in distinctive ways. At one end of the spectrum, the minority opinion, was the 'no-frills' capital proposed by the Victorian Alfred Deakin, three times prime minister, who opted for the 'simplest accommodation . . . the modesty of the wattle and daub, anything that will shelter honourable members from the inclemency of the weather ought to be good enough'; at the other end, the more popular opinion expressed with considerable eloquence by Austin Chapman, the first member for the bellwether New South Wales seat of Eden-Monaro (which contained the Canberra site) only weeks before the casting vote:

> *The Capital cannot be dumped down in a day like a tent. First, the laying out of a great city—a city not for tomorrow, or for the next year, but for all time; a city unique in its beauty and utility with broad avenues intersecting its regular squares, with frequent reservations of grass, flowers, and fountains, with its trees and parks, substantial business houses, and sightly dwellings, its schools, universities, galleries and museums, its monuments and public buildings, its noble rivers and picturesque landscape, its rugged mountains and fertile plains, with Kosciusko in the distance, piercing the sky, and lifting itself like a heavenly dome. These, and many other natural advantages, will offer a noble panorama and a more inspiring contemplation than can possibly be afforded by any other city in the world.*[13]

Chapman's clarion call for quality and commitment may well have proved decisive.

It is hardly surprising that when Hugh Mahon, the Irish-born Minister for Home Affairs in the first Fisher government, barely two months later sent his departmental 'instructions' to District Surveyor Charles Scrivener to commence the preliminary work, he too was caught up in the climate of optimism and aspiration:

> *. . . the surveyor will bear in mind that the Federal Capital should be a beautiful city, occupying a commanding position, with extensive views, and embracing distinctive features which will lend themselves to the*

evolution of a design worthy of the object, not only for the present, but for all time . . .[14]

Clearly, the gap between the design professionals in 1901 and the politicians in 1908 had been bridged.

When King O'Malley took over as Minister in 1910, he readily sang from the same Canberra song sheet. His colleagues, used to his abrupt changes in opinion, were unconcerned that only a few years earlier he had acclaimed the more southern town of Bombala as 'a spot set apart by the Creator to be the Capital of this great Australia'. Once again, O'Malley had been converted anew. As Minister, on 8 September 1910 in the House, he implored his fellow parliamentarians to approach the capital issue 'not as little Australians, but as big Australians', and support the 'Yass–Canberra' region as the future host of 'a city that will be the Gotham of Australia'. Recalling his brief stay in the Monaro a few months earlier, O'Malley felt that in the morning he had 'awakened to a new world'.[15]

In a government that had the first majority in both houses since Federation, the unpredictable if visionary O'Malley had ample time to settle into his portfolio and prioritise those issues which he intended to progress. The recent call from key figures in the design professions, such as John (later Sir John) Sulman, for a 'world-wide competition' to determine the best plan for the new city, was not lost on the American. Talk about 'great' opportunities, 'unique' measures, 'imperishable' monuments built on 'virgin soil', posterity, noblest desires—why, this was his chosen first language. He was raised on hyperbole. He embraced the big stage, the big event. A competition to design the 'Federal City of the Commonwealth of Australia', on O'Malley's watch, must invite the world to participate.

The Minister signalled his intention to go international in a House speech on 7 July 1910 and, shortly after, underscored the transparency of the endeavour with a memorable public statement of intent: 'If an Australian can produce a design, it will be accepted; but we require the best we can get, whether it comes from a Swede or Dane, from Quaker, Shaker or Holy Roller'.[16] But where the American went as an Australian parliamentarian, controversy inevitably followed, and the high-profile design competition proved to be no different. In an otherwise exemplary brief, the judges were not named and, worse, in Section 14 of the 'conditions' the indefatigable Minister took it upon himself to 'adjudicate upon the capital Designs admitted to the competition'. He would make the final decision. There would be no appeals contemplated!

Architectural groups across Australia and throughout the world, including the prestigious Royal Institute of British Architects, were horrified, and made their sentiments known. With his mid-western spurs flying, O'Malley not only rode out the storm, he declared himself utterly vindicated by the quality and number of submissions. His department announced 137 entries from fifteen countries, a large number in itself, but my recent research in the files of the National Archives of Australia has revealed that there may have been as many as 400. The vast majority of these, hopelessly inadequate when measured against the stringent competition criteria, was quickly consigned to the rubbish bin of the Home Affairs department and history—among them, the modest efforts of Adelaide chemist Joseph Edward Coudrey, Lebanon-born Maitland optician Lyon Sab Fares Cavalier, and the two

Marcella Watsons, mother and daughter, wife and unmarried offspring of a Victorian orchardist. For the official field of 137, a decision appears to have been made to include a small, representative cross-section of the multitude of hopefuls, and these included submissions from a clerk, farmer, wool sorter, teacher, accountant, draper, stock broker, salesman, miner, French polisher, butcher, gardener, chemist and a lone astronomer, no doubt reaching for the stars. These token inclusions would not have stayed on the judges' table much longer than the innocent fruits of the Marcella Watsons.

In stark contrast, virtually all the hundred-odd professional entries were submitted by serious players in an impressive, legitimately international field. This was obvious when the official announcement was made by Minister O'Malley, with due ceremony and media attention, on 23 May 1912. Third place went to Entry No. 4, submitted by the Frenchman D. Alfred Agache of Paris, co-founder in 1911 of the Société Française des Urbanistes (for which he served as Secretary-General) and ultimately best-known for what John Reps describes in his monumental study, *Canberra 1912* (1997), as Agache's '*tour de force*', his 'massively detailed master plan for Rio de Janeiro' of 1928. This plan essentially gave us the Rio we know today.

The eighteen drawings comprising Agache's Australian entry—the largest number from any competitor—superb watercolour sketches all, received considerable attention for their aesthetic beauty. One critic in the *Sydney Morning Herald* called it 'a very alluring plan indeed', experts and the general public alike delighting in the bird's-eye view some of the Frenchman's panels afforded them of his city, as if they were 'on board an aeroplane'. Agache allocated a large area of his plan for an airport, and his drawing entitled 'Prospect View of Aerostatic

4.3 One of eighteen drawings comprising Entry No. 4 in the (1911–12) international competition to design Australia's new capital city—the 'exceptionally attractive' entry of Frenchman Hubert Donat Alfred Agache. He loved the new technologies of air travel, and here provides a 'bird's-eye view' of Canberra.

Station—Altitude 1200 Feet' featured both 'airplanes and dirigibles' cruising at a variety of heights. The Australian judges were invited to imagine a technology-savvy city of the future merged into a 'garden city' landscape, as Agache consciously channelled Ebenezer Howard, the Englishman who had presented the Garden City concept to the world not much more than a decade earlier. In summary, this was an imposing entry, from a gifted planner, with a big future in front of him.[17]

Second place in the competition went to Entry No. 18, submitted by Eliel Saarinen, an architect and town planner from Helsinki, Finland, who had already secured a sound reputation on the basis of his design of the Finnish pavilion at the Paris International Exposition in 1900, his Finnish National Museum (1902) and new city plans for Budapest and Tallinn, Estonia (both in 1911). Saarinen's drawings received warm praise from many quarters for their monumentality, 'truly magnificent examples of draughtsmanship' as one commentator put it, but they were also harshly critiqued by others, ostensibly because they were regarded as completely impractical. Couldn't be built. This was a plan with no apparent symbolic connection to either the nation for which it was planned, or the region into which it was to be placed.

The winner, Entry No. 29, had no such fatal flaws. Officially the submission of Walter Burley Griffin, of Chicago, USA, we know (and he publicly acknowledged) it to be a collaborative enterprise with his wife and professional partner, Marion Mahony Griffin. Considering the Australian capital's engaging story to this point, the script to follow could hardly have been bettered. Walt wrote to Minister O'Malley in January 1913, informing him that he had entered the 'Australian event to be my first and last competition, solely because I have for many years greatly admired the bold radical steps in politics and economics which your country has dared to take . . .'[18] Arriving with Marion to stay permanently in Australia, in May 1914, Griffin was steeped in the advanced thinking of American social reformer and radical economist, Henry George (1839–97), who outlined his doctrine of a 'Single Tax' on unimproved land in two classic works of the period: *Progress and Poverty* (1879), which for a time rivalled the Bible in worldwide sales, and *Social Problems* (1883).

The first major lecture Griffin gave in Australia was delivered in 1915 to the Henry George Society in Melbourne, and arguably the two most significant lectures he gave in his entire twenty years in the southern continent were those he reserved for the country's devoted Single-Taxers. In his teenage years in Chicago, we know that Griffin read his *Collected Works* of Henry George with devotion, but he also kept abreast of the progress of the Australian colonies towards nationhood. The Commonwealth's eventual capital-city design competition announcement satisfied a combination of his eclectic readings, interests, passions and extraordinary gifts. Marriage to Marion a few short weeks after the Australian announcement appeared to complete the creative circle, for she brought exquisite architectural rendering skills, a knowledge of non-western design traditions and a breadth of reading that he did not possess to the same heightened degree.

In late 1912, a year before the Australian sojourn became a reality, Griffin clarified his personal motivations in a speech to the Minneapolis Builders' Exchange:

> *We can all be interested in the Australian Federal Capital City not so much for what it is now or will be necessarily, but because of what it stands for: as an opportunity, the best, I believe, so far afforded for an expression of the democratic civic ideal and of all that means in accessibility, freedom, wealth, comfort, conveniences, scale, and splendour.*[19]

Expressing sentiments about Australia almost identical to those of the great American poet Walt Whitman twenty years earlier, Griffin pointed to the new nation as a clean sheet, a *tabula rasa*, the country where the democratic experiment might yet reach its most perfect expression. The extraordinary design that he and Marion created had not only to do justice to the glorious future ahead, it had to stand as a beacon of inspiration in attaining that future. Just over a week after winning the Australian competition, Griffin was interviewed for the *New York Times*, producing perhaps his best-known description of the design which in today's Canberra illuminates the city's central, ceremonial areas. 'I have planned a city,' he announced with just the right blend of intuition, inspiration and arrogance, 'not like any other city in the world. I have planned it not in a way that I expected any government authorities in the world would accept. I have planned an ideal city—a city that meets my ideal of the city of the future.'[20]

It can't be long until Canberra's foundation story, a gift to the nation, gets the recognition it so richly deserves.

Notes

1. James Brunton Stephens, 'The Dominion of Australia (A Forecast)', in Walter Murdoch (compiler), 1924. *A Book of Australasian Verse*, Oxford University Press, London, p.23.
2. See David Headon, 2003. *The Symbolic Role of the National Capital: From Colonial Argument to 21st Century Ideals*, Commonwealth of Australia, Canberra, p.14.
3. See Helen Irving and John Williams, '"The Best Fitted . . . [with] the Greatest Right": Sydney as the Federal Capital', *The New Federalist*, no. 3, June 1999, p.15.
4. See Tessa Milne, 'An Australian Atlantis: Jones' Vision', and Duncan Waterson, '"Progress, Purity and Prohibition": J.G. Drake's Federal Inland Capital Proposal', in *The New Federalist*, no. 3, June 1999, pp. 26–31, 50–5.
5. See John Bannon, 'Queenliest Cities: Australia's capital in the central state', *The New Federalist*, no. 3, June 1999, p. 49.
6. Congress Resolution number 2, 1901. *Proceedings—the Congress of Engineers, Architects, Surveyors, and others interested in the Building of the Federal Capital of Australia, held in Melbourne, in May, 1901*. J.C. Stephens, Melbourne, p. 7.
7. See George Higgins, 1901. 'Inaugural Address', *Proceedings—the Congress*, ibid. pp. 9–12.
8. G. Sydney Jones, 1901. 'Some Thoughts Concerning the Federal City', *Proceedings—the Congress*, ibid. pp. 22–3.
9. C. Bogue Luffmann, 1901. 'The Agricultural, Horticultural and Sylvan Features of a Federal Capital', *Proceedings—the Congress*, ibid. pp. 44–5.
10. See David Headon, 2003. *Symbolic Role of the National Capital*, pp. 23–4.
11. King O'Malley, 19 July 1901. *House of Representatives [HOR]* Robert S. Brain, Melbourne, pp. 2808–9. Also, King O'Malley, 8 October 1903. *HOR*, Robert S. Brain, Melbourne, p. 5934.

12. King O'Malley, ibid.
13. Austin Chapman, 24 September 1908. HOR, J. Kemp, Melbourne, p.390.
14. Hugh Mahon, 21 December 1901. These 'Instructions' of Mahon, the Minister for Home Affairs in the first (Labor) government of Prime Minister Andrew Fisher, were reproduced in *Information, Conditions and Particulars for Guidance in the Preparation of Competitive Designs for the Federal Capital City of the Commonwealth of Australia*, Department of Home Affairs, Melbourne, 30th April 1911, p. 6.
15. King O'Malley, 8 October 1903. *HOR*, Robert S. Brain, Melbourne, p. 5933. Also, King O'Malley, 8 September, 1910. *HOR*, J. Kemp, Melbourne, pp. 2860–1.
16. King O'Malley, 8 September, 1910, ibid. p. 2861.
17. See John W. Reps, 1997. *Canberra 1912: Plans and Planners of the Australian National Capital*, Melbourne University Press, Melbourne, pp. 110–13. For information on Eliel Saarinen, see pp. 132–5.
18. Walter Burley Griffin, 1913. Letter reproduced in Griffin, Dustin (ed.), *The Writings of Walter Burley Griffin*, Cambridge University Press, Cambridge, 2008, p. 36.
19. Walter Burley Griffin, 1912. Letter reproduced in *The Writings of Walter Burley Griffin*, p.30.
20. Walter Burley Griffin, 1912. Letter reproduced in *The Writings of Walter Burley Griffin*, p.23.

5

'A CHOSEN CITY': AMERICANS IN THE CAPITAL

Christopher Vernon

In November 2011, the President of the United States of America Barack Obama made his first official state visit to Australia. Visiting the national capital, he attended a parliamentary dinner at the Great Hall of Parliament House. In his closing remarks, the President noted that he was 'not the first guy from Chicago to come to these parts'. 'A century ago,' he explained, 'Walter Burley Griffin came here with a vision for this city'.[1] The President, however, overlooked another extraordinary American who had also preceded him to Australia's capital: Romaldo Giurgola, the principal architect of the very building in which the President spoke. However, unlike for the city's original authors—Walter and his wife and professional partner Marion Mahony Griffin—and Obama, Giurgola's journey to Canberra began not in Chicago, but an ocean away in Rome.

Recently, the Italian-born architect—known to his friends and colleagues as Aldo—reflected upon his remarkable and life-changing experience of designing and then realising Parliament House.[2] Australia's 1979 design contest for the building was not the first catalyst to put Canberra and the Griffins into Giurgola's architectural imagination. Astonishingly, he first learned of the Australian capital while a university student in Rome, nearly half a century earlier. In 1938, Aldo began studies in architecture at Sapienza-Università di Roma. Mussolini's Palazzo della Civiltà Italiana—a set piece within the dictator's Esposizione Universale Roma city planning initiative to enlarge the Italian capital—had then begun to ominously rise. Around this time, Giurgola's professor Ludovico Quaroni directed his attention to the Griffins' Canberra layout; indeed, a reproduction of it then adorned his classroom's walls. It seems that the American couple's design for an Australian democracy had, paradoxically, found resonance in Fascist Italy. For the young student, the Americans' plan impressed owing to its imagined sympathy with the natural world of a distant land. It was, however, an inauspicious time to begin study; the world was soon again at war and military service intervened. Giurgola eventually graduated in 1948 and next pursued postgraduate studies as a Fulbright Fellow in the United States, where he would remain until Australia beckoned decades later.

There was yet another pre-Parliament House event which emphatically returned Australia to Giurgola's ken. In July 1975, nearly forty years after Quaroni introduced him to Canberra, Australia's National Capital Development Commission (NCDC) launched a design competition for a Walter Burley Griffin Memorial (Marion had then yet to attract recognition beyond 'the hand that held the pencil'). This commemorative work, envisaged to be positioned atop Mount Ainslie, was intended to mark the centenary of Griffin's birth, as well as his native United States' bicentennial the next year. The Walter Burley Griffin Memorial Design Competition was conducted in two stages.

Along with the NCDC, the contest was sponsored by the National Memorials Committee and the Administrator of US Bicentennial Activities. The NCDC planned to complete construction of the winning design by 24 November 1976, the centenary of Griffin's birth. Jurors included town planner and Griffin scholar Peter Harrison, the NCDC's Tony Powell, and celebrated American town planning authority Edmund N. Bacon. Five entries advanced to the second stage (24 November–13 February 1976). Disappointingly, the Mitchell/Giurgola Associates (MGA) submission did not attract a prize.

Robert Crane's design emerged as the second-stage winner, although it is unclear precisely when. In the political upheaval surrounding the November 1975 dismissal of the Whitlam government, the project soon languished. By April 1976, with a new government in place, cost had become a pressing concern. That month, *Architecture Australia* reported that the government had 'shelved' the memorial, laconically assessing that Griffin would be remembered only 'if we can afford it'.

News of the project's demise apparently didn't travel fast. In May, a hemisphere away, the *Journal of the American Institute of Architects* reported that the memorial's ground breaking would be on 4 July and the finished work unveiled on 24 November 1976. Back in Australia, the Griffin memorial was not, apparently, completely dead. In June 1976, *Architecture Australia* noted that documentation of Crane's prize-winning design was going ahead to 'bring [it] to a stage where work on building can begin quickly when the Government decides that it can afford to have the memorial'. Whether or not this actually happened is unclear; it may well be that the fully documented design lies forgotten among the NCDC's voluminous records. Nonetheless, in the August edition of *Architecture Australia*, the NCDC, likely in response to criticism of its decision to shelve the project, 'point[ed] out that while the memorial has been dropped from the current financial program, it is in the Commission's five year program as normal work'. More than thirty-five years later, Walter and Marion are still waiting.

The MGA entry—indicative of the landscape sensibility that would later pervade Parliament House's design—comprised an assemblage of monolithic pylons, clad with text-inscribed glass and mirrors, composed, in his words, 'in such a way as to get you to see the city and the configurations of the land'. The mirrors, through their reflection and refraction, ethereally 'deconstruct' and re-project the Griffins' crystalline geometry. 'So,' the architect explains, 'Griffin comes into the equation—a continuous relation between the national land and the mountains, as in Mahony's drawing.'

Curiously, the Griffin memorial was not the first time Aldo had made a design within the wider context of a Southern Hemisphere national capital. At the time of the Australian competition, he was at work constructing a cultural centre, the Casa Thomas Jefferson (1973), at Brasília, Canberra's Brazilian counterpart, designed capital and successor. Indeed, some of Parliament House's germinal seeds were first sown on Brazilian soil. American professional journal *Architectural Forum* observed that 'unlike most [buildings] at Brasília', the Casa Thomas Jefferson 'focusses inward', organised around a courtyard garden. 'The architects,' the magazine continued, 'liken the intriguing garden to the scale, informality and tightly knit quality of Rio [de Janeiro]'s squatters' settlement; and will reinforce these qualities through the painterly use of colors on the stucco exteriors—pinks, violets and greens relating to the pungent red earth color [of Brasília's landscape setting]—in an additional effort to break away from the sterility of Brasília.'[3] Parliament House would later similarly feature interior and exterior courtyards and draw upon the landscape for its chromatic references. When visiting Casa Thomas Jefferson in 2012, I was informed, in testament to the building's significance, that it had won heritage protection from the Brazilian government.

Owing to the international prominence he had achieved by the late 1970s, Giurgola was initially invited to serve as an adjudicator for the Parliament House competition. Wishing instead to participate in the contest himself, he declined the invitation. In 1980, Mitchell/Giurgola & Thorp's design, with Aldo as its principal author and Peter G. Rolland, the landscape architect, won the contest. Their scheme's sensitive response to and accentuation of the Griffins' original plan was central to its success. In the couple's layout, Mount Kurrajong (today Capital Hill) was to become the site for a ceremonial 'Capitol', a building they envisaged to enshrine the achievements of the Australian people. Now, however, the government controversially reallocated the summit as the site for Parliament House. For some, this decision to symbolically displace the 'People' in favour of the 'Government' seemed to eliminate the possibility of ever realising the Griffins' vision. Giurgola's design, however, innovatively reconstructed the hill as architecture; citizens could climb earthen ramps, literally walking atop Parliament House and their government (in the aftermath of 11 September 2001, however, this practice was, sadly, curtailed and the ramps barricaded). Encircled by gardens, Parliament House is at once landscape and architecture or, more literally, landscape architecture. A monumental flagpole structure, its pyramidal form evocative of the Griffins' unrealised 'Capitol', crowns the remarkable ensemble and is today an iconic element which punctuates the national capital's skyline.

Although unintentional, the design's careful scrutiny and detailed consideration of the Griffins' plan also served to renew professional attention to the couple's layout, largely dismissed in the post-war era as merely 'history'.

5.1 Pencil etching by Romaldo Giurgola (Aldo) of the view along Anzac Parade towards the new Parliament House.

In 1985, Giurgola moved to Australia to orchestrate construction of Parliament House on site. After the building's completion in 1988, Aldo, like the Griffins before him, chose to remain in Australia and invest himself in the national capital. Seduced by Canberra's landscape beauty, he now concerned himself with conserving and enhancing the capital's distinctiveness, a passion that would prove ongoing.

In 2010, an exhibition was mounted at Parliament House to commemorate Giurgola's ninetieth birthday—the display and its contents no less elegant than the venue.[4] Most of the drawings exhibited were executed with humble pencil on paper and ranged from elevations and plans to expansive exterior perspectives, including ones of Parliament House. Not unlike Marion Griffin's earlier Canberra competition renderings (1911), Giurgola's Parliament House views were undoubtedly a persuasive force in the later contest's outcome (1980). In harsh contrast to our twenty-first-century world of computer-generated, hyper-realistic and often sterile architectural imagery, Giurgola's renderings—like Marion's and despite the passage of time—exude a humane intimacy.

•

Throughout his nearly thirty years in Australia, Aldo has vigilantly monitored and routinely commented publicly upon the national capital's development. Although now effectively retired, he most recently physically accentuated Canberra's landscape through the design transformation of a plantation of oak trees at York Park from simply an arboreal feature into elegant, habitable parkland. Aldo conceived this metamorphosis in association with his long-time landscape architecture collaborators, Mervyn Dorrough and the late Peter Britz, recently retired directors of Redbox Design Group in Canberra, and Pamille Berg of Pamille Berg Consulting.

The 'new' park actually has a lengthy history. Its genesis came in 1927 with the planting of a single tree. That year, HRH Prince Albert, Duke of York, opened Australia's Provisional Parliament House. Contrary to popular belief, the city's designers Walter Burley Griffin and Marion Mahony Griffin also witnessed the spectacle.

Opening Parliament, however, wasn't the Duke's only task. The next day, with far less fanfare, he made a ceremonial contribution to the capital's emergent landscape. On a windswept plain at the junction of Federal Avenue and Capitol Circle (later renamed King's Avenue and State Circle), the Duke planted an English Oak tree, supplied by the Royal Botanic Gardens at Kew, in London. The future King's Oak remained a solitary tree adorning an otherwise open paddock until 1931. That year, as Australia languished in the Great Depression, the Commonwealth government funded planting of additional trees as relief work. With the Duke's tree as cue, seventy-eight additional English Oaks were planted on a twelve-metre grid, establishing a plantation nearly two hectares in extent.

The plantation was largely forgotten to all, other than local residents, until 2003, when the site was threatened with redevelopment. Commonwealth Heritage Listing the next year rescued the plantation and, in 2007, the National Capital Authority commissioned Giurgola and his landscape architects to conserve and transform it. In 2011, after a two-million-dollar redevelopment, the York Park North Oak Plantation reopened. Beneath the plantation's almost continuous canopy and eschewing the all too familiar picturesque, Giurgola and his colleagues organised the undulating ground with a faceted geometry, foiling the rigid tree grid. Finely crafted walls of local stone delineate the park's limits, evoking, in the architect's words, 'the memory of walls in the English countryside, in sympathy with the oaks'. The wall profiles follow the five-metre drop in the level of the land to the north, enabling panoramic views throughout the site. Within the park, episodic paths, designed to be punctuated with interpretative signage, lead to seating areas accentuated with low walls. The park features a central gathering place to accommodate, for instance, concerts. One must also remember that, unlike their Australian counterparts, English Oaks are deciduous, lending the park a dynamic quality. After shedding their leaves at winter's approach, the oak branches, along with the lines of the exposed walls and the footpaths, again as Giurgola put it, 'all become like the signs of an abstract drawing'. Adding another layer to the plantation's history, Giurgola himself planted an oak on his ninetieth birthday. The former plantation is now a place of peace and contemplation, nestled within Canberra's ceremonial heart. As he recently explained to me, Giurgola had 'always been surprised by the wonderful silence' found in the plantation. 'Automobiles move along the adjoining avenues without noise; a helicopter flies overhead without being heard. Silence is truly the most precious thing we are left with today, and this is the first gift we receive from York Park'. Hopefully, this will not be Aldo's Canberra swan song.

•

I first followed in the Griffins' and Romaldo's footsteps from the United States to Canberra in 1993. Once there, I sought the architect out at his Manuka office. Not only did he generously entertain my queries for the better part of two hours, but he also gave me a personal tour of Parliament House—known to me until then only through photographs. In early 1995, I returned, then believing temporarily, to teach landscape architecture at the University of Canberra. Unknown to me at the time, some five years later, I—acting as Design Advisor to the National Capital Authority (an appointment made owing to my extensive knowledge of the Griffins' lives and works)—would be privileged to work alongside him on the 'Griffin Legacy' project, an initiative which explored the relevance of the Griffins' original vision for

5.2 Architect Romaldo Giurgola next to Walter

the national capital in the twenty-first century. Although unanticipated at first, like Aldo, I also chose to remain in Australia.

I have always felt a special affinity with Aldo; Canberra profoundly and unexpectedly redirected both our lives, eventually prompting mutual relocation from the United States to Australia, and culminating with Australian citizenship. I initially experienced Giurgola's work at first hand in 1982. Then an architecture student, I set out on a pilgrimage to St. Louis to visit Louis Sullivan's Wainwright building (1890–91). Sullivan, also the Griffins' intellectual mentor and muse, continues to loom large in my pantheon of architect greats. Reaching the Missouri metropolis on the Mississippi after half a day's drive from Chicago, I found my way to the rust-coloured, terracotta-clad, ten-storey building. Named for its client, the Wainwright was originally conceived as a commercial office block. Now, however, it had taken on public dimension, accommodating state government offices and, more palpably, gaining additions and extensions (1981). I was overwhelmed by the new structures' disciplined, restrained deference to the Sullivan masterwork. No less impressive was that the additions were configured to form courtyards and plazas, making a continuous transition between old and new. Rills and pools, reminiscent of those to be found at the Alhambra, linked and interconnected interior and exterior. Encountering these new constructions was an epiphany; my focus on Sullivan and the past had come at the expense of the present. Research upon my return revealed the authors of this elegant ensemble to be MGA and that victory in a national design competition (1974) had won the commission.[5] As I would later discover, courtyard pool and rill devices reappear in Parliament House. Similarly, in his design of the new St Patrick's Cathedral at Parramatta (2002), one nothing short of magisterial, Giurgola reapplied his exquisite spoliation technique, respectfully fusing old with new.

In one conversation with me, Giurgola astutely identified that 'behind the [Griffins' Canberra] drawings is a strong perception of the humanity of the place'. Humanity—as well as humility—is no less discernible throughout Romaldo Giurgola's own distinguished oeuvre.

As first revealed to me at St. Louis, Aldo's architecture is, foremost, humane; it sensitively considers, responds to and reinterprets what preceded it. Or, as Aldo recently put it to me, for him architecture begins with consideration of 'content', not form. His work is antithetical to, for instance, the bombastic, if not narcissistic, species of architecture to be found nearby on the Acton Peninsula. As epitomised by Parliament House, Giurgola's buildings are timeless and transcend fashion.

Writing in 1912, under the spell of Marion Griffin's Canberra competition renderings, one critic rhapsodised: 'the buildings are spread so thinly on the ground, are so masked with trees, and are so small relative to the majestic roll of the terrain, that you see, not them, but Australia'. The same could be said of the view today from atop Mount Ainslie, down the Griffins' Land Axis (now Anzac Parade) to Australia's now iconic Parliament House. Along with Sydney's Opera House, Parliament House is, arguably, one of the very few Australian buildings of truly international significance.

Acknowledgements

This chapter is a revision and expansion of my earlier pieces, 'Landscape of Contemplation', *Indesign*, no. 48, March–May 2012, pp. 192–4 and 'Lines that Speak', *Architecture Australia*, 100, no. 2, March 2011, pp. 25–6. Unreferenced quotations from Aldo were drawn from numerous interviews with him throughout more than a decade, most recently at his home in January 2012. I remain grateful to him for the gift of his friendship. I also thank Pamille Berg for her ongoing assistance with my work on Aldo.

Notes

1 See 'After Dinner Remarks by President Obama at Parliamentary Dinner' at: http://www.whitehouse.gov/the-press-office/2011/11/16/after-dinner-remarks-president-obama-parliamentary-dinner (accessed 28 December 2012). Also see 'No Better Friends', *Canberra Times*, 16 November 2011.

2 Romaldo, along with his colleagues Pamille Berg and Hal Guida, participated in the National Archives of Australia symposium *Designing for Canberra* on 14 November 2010.

3 'Foreign Intrigue', *Architectural Forum*, vol. 138, June 1973, p. 10.

4 The exhibition *Lines that Speak: Architectural Drawings of Romaldo Giurgola* was displayed from 3 September–31 October 2010.

5 The project was executed in association with St. Louis architects Hastings + Chivetta.

6

THE VIEW FROM MOUNT AINSLIE

Andrew Sayers

Ascending Mount Ainslie, we notice that our walk up the track is annotated with texts.

At the foot of the mountain, behind the Australian War Memorial, a side track leads to a bronze plaque set into a stone: 'Remembering the Aboriginal People who served in the Australian Forces'. This plaque is in the midst of a tract of bush named to mark the sixtieth anniversary of the signing of the Armistice in 1978. The naming of the southern slope of the hill 'Remembrance Nature Park' was at the instigation of Honor Thwaites, a prominent moral and environmental crusader in Canberra, proud of her role, described on another introductory sign, as 'Park Carer'.[1]

On the track up the hill, there are bronze plaques, set in concrete implants, describing battle incidents on the Kokoda Track in 1942, as though Mount Ainslie were a simulacrum of jungle battlefield terrain in Papua New Guinea. The plaques bear contour maps of the Owen Stanley Range with the disconcerting inscription 'You are here'.[2]

In the languidly looping middle part of the ascent, there is a kind of Australian haiku in botanical labels; 'Scribbly Gum . . . Narrow-leafed

Bitter Pea . . . Drooping She-oak . . . Golden Everlasting'. The path goes towards the heavens.

On the summit parapet there is more to read: solid grey plaques commemorating Sir John Butters and Sir John Overall and signs charting the development of the city and describing the Griffin Plan. From this vantage point on Mount Ainslie, Canberra spreads before us, evoking a visual memory of the dream-city of Walter Burley Griffin, drawn on delicate silk by his wife Marion Mahony Griffin. It brings to mind Judith Wright's 'Brief Notes on Canberra':

This basin in the hills
holds a lens of clear air.
Day looks down through it
like a blue-eyed jeweller.[3]

Almost every part of this vista has some association for me, personal and professional. The personal ones are all over the place; the professional ones more focused—the National Gallery of Australia, where I began my Canberra career in 1985, the National Portrait Gallery (its low-slung roof barely visible) and the National Museum of Australia, a flash of orange on the right-hand side of the composition.[4] (From my office at the National Gallery the symmetry of Mount Ainslie had a Japanese perfection.)

Having been part of the life of these three cultural institutions, as well as having spent many hours in the National Library and other edifices framed in the view, I have sometimes pondered the question: How did we end up with the suite of cultural institutions we have in the capital? Is there logic to it? Over the past century, there have been many proposals for cultural institutions that have gone nowhere.

The Griffins were the first to see Canberra as a place of cultural institutions and their idea for the city encompassed a different group to the one we have a hundred years later. As part of the original competition for the design of the national capital in 1911, the brief allowed for sites for a national art gallery and library, a museum and a national theatre. In his winning design, Griffin expanded on this core of civic buildings and proposed not one but two art galleries—paired galleries of the graphic and plastic arts; and paired museums of natural history and archaeology. In keeping with this cultural broadening, Griffin imagined the national theatre as both a theatre and opera house. Furthermore, he proposed a zoo with nearby baths and gymnasia.

At various times in Canberra's history, enthusiasts have floated other ideas for cultural institutions—from natural history collections, technology museums and an air-and-space museum. In 1965, when Canberra's built landscape was well advanced, the National Capital Development Commission (NCDC) developed a bold vision for the future of the capital. It included a scheme for a national centre comprising five elements: a national art gallery, two major museums, a great exhibition hall and a monument to symbolise Australia's achievements in time of peace. This last element was a conscious riposte to the place of the Australian War Memorial in the formation of our national consciousness. Of the two museums proposed by the NCDC in 1965, one was concerned with Australia's geography, natural history and Aboriginal Australia, the other was a history museum devoted to

Australia post-1788, having an emphasis on technological and scientific development with 'perhaps a glimpse into the future'.[5]

When the federal government asked a committee of enquiry chaired by Peter Pigott to report on Australia's museums in 1974, further ideas for museums were floated.[6] The Pigott Report, completed in 1975, recommended the establishment of a Gallery of Aboriginal Australia and a National Museum of Australia, yet the committee found merit in only three of the many specialist museum ideas that had been put forward. The report recommended that 'early priority be given to a national maritime museum in Sydney and to a national aviation museum at a growth centre such as Albury–Wodonga, and that later consideration be given to locating a Gallery or Museum of Australian Biography . . .' A National Maritime Museum was duly established in Sydney, but the recommendation for a national aviation museum didn't get off the ground.

Even as they recommended it, the members of Pigott's committee did not express any urgency about the establishment of a museum devoted to biography. Indeed, there was a certain ambivalence. Committee members suggested that if the Gallery of Biography were conceived as 'a kind of national pantheon' it should be sited in the centre of Canberra. They were at pains to point out that in making this proposal they were reluctant to foster chauvinism. Nonetheless, they concluded that the proposed 'Gallery of Biography could be a useful, simple focus for nationalist sentiments'.

The opening of the National Portrait Gallery, some two decades after the Pigott Report, fulfilled the aspiration for a museum with biography as its organising principle. When I took up the role as the first director of the National Portrait Gallery in 1998, some of the ambivalence expressed by the Pigott Committee was still in evidence. Indeed the ambivalence is fundamental to the very idea of national portrait galleries. Should a National Portrait Gallery be a pantheon (principally including figures worthy of emulation) or should it be more truly reflective of history in which the human players exhibit all the traits of human nature, good and bad?

The National Portrait Gallery we now have in Australia very much tends towards an inclusive presentation. The historical significance of the portrait subject is taken as the single most important criterion for inclusion. Nonetheless, in proposing portraits for the National Portrait Gallery, proponents and subjects often express the view that to be included is a form of honour. Some of the earlier associations of the pantheon still cling to the portrait gallery concept.

The first iteration of the National Portrait Gallery was a dedicated display space in Old Parliament House, under the aegis of the National Library of Australia. The gallery had been established following concerted lobbying by philanthropists Gordon and Marilyn Darling, who sponsored a travelling exhibition of portraits in 1992–93, entitled *Uncommon Australians*. The subtitle of that exhibition—*Towards an Australian Portrait Gallery*—was a clear indication that the exhibition was intended to serve as a model on which a future National Portrait Gallery might be based.

The history of the idea of the National Portrait Gallery and of the Darlings' continued commitment to the idea and their material support for it is another story,[7] yet their aspirations for the gallery and its wider *raison d'être* are relevant to my theme.

As a latecomer, joining the already established national gallery, museum, library, archives and war museum, the National Portrait

Gallery took its place among the suite of national cultural institutions 'telling the Australian story'. It was conscious of the particular and singular way in which it fits with the suite of cultural institutions. In focusing on individual lives it deals with specificity and works against generalisation.

At various times in its history, the gallery has distinguished itself from other presentations in its insistence that it is not primarily concerned with 'social history'. Indeed the gallery's principal organising idea—biography—implies life-spans that resist definition by historical era or that can be neatly pushed into the confining compartments of broader social currents. While it is an aim of the gallery to represent people in the full flight of the activities for which they are famous, this is not always easy to define, let alone represent.

'National identity' is an idea associated with Canberra institutions but I would argue that this is an unexamined expectation of visitors, rather than an explicit part of their presentations. When the new National Portrait Gallery building was opened in 2008, the words 'national identity' were not used by the gallery to describe its concerns; yet, as its visitors' book will attest, people visiting the gallery find manifestations of 'national identity' throughout the displays. This is a not unreasonable expectation of Canberra.

In 2010, I moved from the National Portrait Gallery to the National Museum of Australia. This gave me a particular insight into the contrast and the similarities between these two entities. While the National Museum's mandate can legitimately be described as social history museum, it, too, is compelled to confront the specificity of individual experience. Consistently the museum has personalised its presentations: 'Milo Dunphy's Pram'; 'Dulcie Greeno's Necklace';

'Ron Muncaster's Platform Shoe' and so on. Many of the objects in the museum's collection appear to speak to a sense of 'collective memory'. Yet this somewhat slippery concept is something brought to the museum by visitors, rather than an explicit idea expressed in the displays. The similarities between the National Portrait Gallery and the National Museum were less obvious to me in 2010 than the dissimilarities. Not only was the collection much bigger, its complexity and range made the collecting of portraits seem, by contrast, extremely simple and pure. The 'cultural baggage', too, of the museum was heavier than that of the uncontroversial National Portrait Gallery, both in conceptual and physical terms. In March 2011, as the National Museum of Australia celebrated the tenth anniversary of the opening of its building, I felt that the dream of the museum had been realised only partially. In the public mind—at least as it was reflected in media commentary—there were two dominant ideas about the museum that persisted. Many people saw the museum's short history only as a story of public controversy over frontier conflict; or to use the shorthand of the day, they viewed the museum as a combatant in the 'history wars'. For many other commentators the museum was the butt of architectural critique.

I sensed that attitudes on both of these fronts were changing. The debate around the veracity of the historical record relating to colonial dispossession had lost its previous ferocity. Furthermore, the voices of visitors who enjoyed the museum's bold architecture now balanced those of detractors. In a speech coinciding with the tenth anniversary of the opening of the National Museum of Australia, I tried to put aside both the museum's history and its building in order to find a way to describe its collection and my sense of its uniqueness among Australia's cultural institutions. I argued that a fundamental role for the Museum is to:

> *make sense of some of the enduring stories that have contributed to our uniqueness and distinctiveness as a nation. In Australia, the most powerful stories are stories of arriving and the acts of creation released by arrival in a new place . . . If there is a national narrative in Australia it is about place. All of our national stories will in some way express themselves in relation to specific places—tracts of country, rivers, localities, villages or cities.* [8]

In one way or another, sense of place in Australian stories informs all of the cultural institutions set in Canberra's basin in the hills. It strikes me that this sense of place is twofold. In 'telling the Australian story' cultural institutions are telling the stories of Australian places. Stories can be re-told and represented in many forms but they cannot be uprooted from the places in which they have occurred. On another level, the place of Canberra itself is significant, symbolically.

Attachment to place is the closest we can find to a universal in Australian experience. Place informs the National Portrait Gallery as powerfully as it does the National Museum of Australia. The National Portrait Gallery building opened in 2008 was designed by Richard Johnson as a consciously 'Australian' building. Unlike the National Museum of Australia's building, with its embedded codes and references to Australian national identity—seen in its most extreme expression in the Garden of Australian Dreams—the signals are more subtle in the National Portrait Gallery. For example, the building's form and timber truss elements are references to the iconic Australian woolshed. In its use of timber and stone, and in the landscape treatment, the architecture expresses a federal idea—sourcing representatives from each state and territory and bringing them together in a unified ensemble in Canberra. The only precedents for such a deliberate federalism of materials were the 1963 Law Courts Building (Supreme Court of the ACT) in which the six courtrooms use state-themed timber selections for joinery, and in the Parliament House building.

When the new National Portrait Gallery was opened at the end of 2008, I wanted to state explicitly the connectedness of Australian experience through place. The first exhibition *Open Air: Portraits in the Landscape* was based on the premise that while other countries with national portrait galleries could find national narratives through changes in political structures over time, Australia could best find a series of national narratives through different attitudes to the landscape. For Indigenous Australians these attitudes are clearly fundamental in defining identity. They can be seen in the works of artists such as the bark painters of Arnhem Land. In the work of successive generations of the Marika family of Yirrkala, the connection between places, ancestral stories and the law can be seen with real clarity, even if some of the meanings of the painters' iconography are hidden. Settler Australian attitudes to place were explored, too, in the *Open Air* exhibition—the paintings of Sidney Nolan (of quasi-mythical encounters with the interior, the Burke and Wills series) and Arthur Boyd's memories of Port Phillip Bay, painted in London. These paintings were included in order to impress upon the viewer the many ways, subtle and obvious, in which place can be present in the work of artists most powerfully through individual memory and engagement with myth.

Open Air included paintings by Arthur Boyd made in Canberra during his stint in the city as Creative Fellow at the Australian National University in 1971–72. Boyd's statement about living in the suburb of Garran expressed a truth about living and working in Canberra that can be so easily felt by the longer term resident:

> *I could walk into the country in five minutes. It was quite marvellous: there was this undulating, rolling quality. And the weather—the blueness of the sky . . .*[9]

As we descend from the summit of Mount Ainslie, we are yet again in the bush zone where the Australian War Memorial spreads its memorialising force. The War Memorial's place in the Australian imagination was best summed up in Charles Bean's 1948 description of the Australians whose record is there memorialised; 'Here is their spirit, *in the heart of the land they loved . . .*' Bean's phrase has justly become famous, not simply because it sums up the reason for the Australian War Memorial's existence with memorable conciseness but, I think, because it embraces a series of ideas about Canberra. As a place, Canberra shares qualities with much of regional Australia—a place in which the natural world, the bush and the quality of the light—are never far away. Yet Canberra is set apart from those other places in that it possesses a symbolic quality that cannot be found anywhere else. The metaphor of 'heart' is both a description of interiority and emotional locus. Everyone involved with cultural institutions in Canberra is aware that a body, a nation, spreads out from here in all directions.

6.1 The Hall of Memory at the Australian War Memorial.

Notes

1 Anne Brennan, 'Lest We Forget: Military Myths, Memory, and Canberra's Aboriginal and Torres Strait Islander Memorial', *Memory Connection,* vol. 1, no. 1, 2011.

2 The plaques are part of a project commemorating Australian military history instigated by the Melbourne periodontist Dr Ross Bastiaan AM. Bastiaan's work is described on the website www.plaques.satlink.com.au.

3 Judith Wright, extract from *Fourth Quarter*, 1977. Angus & Robertson, Sydney.

4 The author was Curator of Australian Drawings at the National Gallery of Australia until 1996 when he became Assistant Director (Collections). From 1998 until 2010, he was the inaugural Director of the National Portrait Gallery. In 2010, he was appointed as Director of the National Museum of Australia.

5 National Capital Development Commission, 1964. *The Future Canberra: A long range plan for land use and civic design,* Commonwealth Government Printer, Canberra.

6 The report of the *Committee of Inquiry on Museums and National Collections*, chaired by Peter Pigott, can be found on the website of the National Museum of Australia: www.nma.gov.au. See also Anne-Marie Condé, *The orphans of government*, The Committee of Inquiry on Museums and National Collections (The Pigott Report), 1974–5, in Des Griffin and Leon Paroissien (eds), *Understanding Museums*, e-publication accessible through National Museum of Australia website.

7 For a fuller rendition of the history of the National Portrait Gallery see the introduction in Sarah Engledow, 2008. *The Companion*, National Portrait Gallery, Canberra.

8 National Press Club, Canberra, 16 March 2011.

9 Quoted by Mary Eagle in *Three Creative Fellows: Sidney Nolan, Arthur Boyd, Narritjin Maymuru*, 2007. Drill Hall Gallery, Australian National University, Canberra.

7

A GREAT PLACE TO RAISE (AUSTRALIAN) KIDS

Shanti Sumartojo

I didn't know anything about Canberra before I moved here. I'm not sure I even knew it was the capital. In fact, I didn't really know anything about the rest of Australia, either, and my impressions had been conditioned by years in Indonesia, from where Australia appeared rich, white, orderly and reasonable, and in the United Kingdom, from where it appeared sunny, relaxed, filled with deadly wildlife and Very Far Away. Taken as a whole, this was overwhelmingly positive, and the decision to move to Australia was an uncomplicated combination of pragmatism and romance. We picked a destination from the *Lonely Planet* descriptions, bought one-way tickets, and arrived in a blissful Melbourne summer that quickly took the edge off my Edinburgh tan. Fresh to the country, still working out what my Australia would be, Melbourne seemed to fit the urban shopping list quite well: multicultural, convivial, great food, plenty of work opportunities and, important after Scottish winters, hot. But an opportunity came up in Canberra that was too good to turn down, so we packed a hire car and drove down the Hume Highway to our new home.

Disgruntlement set in early. From the late-night perspective of a slowly deflating air mattress, we asked hard questions about why we had come here and whether we should stay. It was bad enough that there didn't seem to be any pubs, public transport or decent shops, but where were all the people? When I failed the personality section of the public service entrance exam, it was just another indication of Canberra's unsuitability (rather than my own). We promised each other we'd get the most out of the city for a few years, and then move on to somewhere that suited us better. That was in 1999.

Like many other people, the deep ambivalence about the city that characterised my first years in Canberra was gradually softened by work, study, children and the practice of everyday life. Canberra framed the serious adult business of starting a family and building a professional identity, and it has helped shape how I understand myself, Australia, and my intellectual preoccupations of identity, nationhood, place and history. But a determined core of resistance remains and, even though the shops are better and I've found both pubs and people that I really enjoy, I'll never be that awkward noun, I tell myself, a 'Canberran'.

Despite this, I can't help but grind my teeth slightly at the received wisdom that Canberra is 'not the real Australia'. Not only does this cliché seem to fall easily from the lips of taxi drivers the length and breadth of the country, but even those who live their own very real lives here seem to be suspicious of their own experience. But why should the lives of people who live in Canberra be any more (or less) Australian that others'? Residents of this city may be better educated, less sexist, wealthier and more often employed than the national average, but only slightly. Like countless of our compatriots, many of us work in offices, buy groceries, take the children to school and shake our fists at the television. Why should we compare less favourably to a national ideal of 'Australianness'?

7.1 David Tolley's Play Sculpture, 1970, commissioned by the National Capital Development Commission.

I think the answer to this lies in Canberra's landscape, real and imagined, national and personal. This landscape can be best understood as a tension between the ideological, abstract and powerful on the one hand and the personal and quotidian on the other. Other authors in this collection talk about the 'imagined' city of Canberra and what this means. These imaginings are often national, and as a scholar of national identity and urban geography, the combination of Canberra's grand national narratives, writ explicitly and apparently inflexibly within the layout of its central district, with the cosy, lived-in domesticity of its ubiquitous suburbs, has always fascinated me. The experience of having children, a profound undertaking by any definition, reshaped the city for me. Children produce their own versions of Canberra, and the implications are not only for families, but for Australian national identity more generally.

Where are all the people?

Canberra's central built environment, the so-called Parliamentary Triangle, is dotted with buildings housing national institutions. The architecture of these structures isn't uniformly welcoming, the term 'Brutalist' not a long stretch in describing some of them. Many of them were designed and constructed in the 1960s and 1970s, and they have an uncompromising angularity that can be hard to warm to, the lofty ideals of clean, efficient Modernism notwithstanding. Certainly they look formal, and this impression is reinforced by their careful placement in relation to one another, the spaces in between filled with sculptures or grassed areas that appear deliberate without clear clues as to purpose. This is not an architectural landscape on a human scale, but one that looks cogent and comprehensible from the perspective of an aeroplane or on a map.

The functions of these buildings are also formal. In addition to several august national cultural institutions, the Triangle contains the seriousness of the Parliament itself, and the government buildings housing the even more serious departments of Finance and Treasury, among others. It is also peppered with monuments and memorials, most obviously on the north side of the lake on Anzac Parade, not strictly speaking part of the Parliamentary Triangle, but closely linked to it both visually and ideologically.

The placement of these monuments is not accidental, and is regulated by a set of guidelines administered by the National Capital Authority. These stipulate that different areas of the Parliamentary Triangle are reserved for different types of works: there are specific zones set aside for honouring achievements in the 'Humanities and Sciences', 'Arts and Civics', and public service. The area around Old Parliament House is reserved for monuments related to Federation, and commemorations of foreigners are not allowed at all, except on the grounds of the relevant embassies, many of which are to the south and west. Anzac Parade is reserved for military memorials, and these march northward to the sombre dome of the Australian War Memorial crouching at the foot of Mount Ainslie. Like the city itself, this almost Victorian approach to categorising and controlling this nationally recognised space makes a lot of sense on a map, but isn't easily legible from the ground. The plan's logic, in other words, doesn't make obvious sense to the people who inhabit and animate it.

Something, therefore, about Canberra's central districts isn't quite on the human scale. Even getting there from the main shopping area in Civic on foot, as many visitors attempt, requires a confusing trip to the far side of Lake Burley Griffin. This begins obviously enough, but is soon obscured by fast-moving traffic darting around unexpected curves in the road. On a sunny day, the blinding concrete of Commonwealth Bridge is disorienting and bewildering, and pedestrians straggle out along the two kilometres or so of this journey, hats askew, upside down maps flapping in the breeze off the lake. Once reached, the relative calm of the Triangle itself is a drawn-out walk in the hot glare with distances that look much shorter than they turn out to be. Children wilt and drag their feet. Adults stagger for the cool interiors of the cultural institutions, making straight for the toilets and the bubbler. There can be brief moments of clarity as the eye is drawn in one direction across the lake and up Anzac Parade to the War Memorial, and in the other to Old and then new Parliament House. The observer glimpses a brief mirage of the Griffins' plan, the structure and symbolism of the plan momentarily evident. Suddenly you can imagine the logic of the layout despite having just suffered as a result of it.

One response to the illegibility of central Canberra's 'landscape of power' would be to say that it wasn't designed for people, but rather for institutions, monuments and memorials. But these buildings represent something about Australia, can be said to 'produce' a vision of Australia that is ideological—and by this I mean these structures tell us who we are meant to be, and what hierarchies of power shape our national identities. This is reflected in the institutional nomenclature—the *National* Gallery, the *National* Library, the *National* Museum of *Australia*, the *Australian* High Court, the *Australian* War Memorial—and their grouping together in the capital city. Their concentration in one apprehensible mass helps them to augment each other, like a group of teenagers, as if to say 'I'll do it if you will'. Taken alone, or spread throughout a larger area, the impact would not be the same.

Research on national identity has quite a lot to say about the relationship between the official, 'top-down' depiction of the nation exemplified in places like the Parliamentary Triangle, and the lived, everyday experience and use of those environments by residents and visitors. A good starting point is Benedict Anderson's notion of the nation as an 'imagined community'[1], in which not everyone knows each other, but they still understand themselves as co-nationals. Anderson explored some of the specific ways in which the national imaginary is generated and popularised, identifying, among other things, the categorising power of the 'map, census and museum' as important ways that unitary national identities are created. The Griffins' plan and the cultural institutions in central Canberra fulfil these functions nicely.

Others scholars similarly emphasise the structural aspects of national identity. British sociologist Anthony Smith wrote that the nation has 'objective characteristics constitutive of a national identity independent of individual consciousness'[2]. In other words, it is both abstract and powerful, and the individual has little scope to intervene in it. Eric Hobsbawm and Terence Ranger contributed the idea of the 'invention of tradition', explaining how powerful groups work through social and political structures to serve their own interests by using popular ideas, values and symbols to build a national culture that bridges different languages and ethnicities[3]. They identified the important role of numerous public monuments, including war memorials, commemorative statues and public buildings to reflect and reinforce narratives of national power. These scholars, along with many others, formulated ways of understanding national identity as determined by elites, enforced through powerful institutions, far beyond the reach of the individual, that were monolithic and inflexible. Written mostly by men with a direct experience of the European national upheavals of the mid- to late-twentieth century, these accounts all concentrate on structure and emphasise an 'objective' cultural form of national identity, implying that such identities are fixed and that all members of the political community agree (or at least don't have the capacity to argue).

The bricks-and-mortar symbolism of central Canberra would appear to support these ways of understanding national identity. So what is the significance of this inescapably national landscape? What fixed truths does it tell us about ourselves? Looking at Canberra, we could conclude that, as a nation, we value military sacrifice, the institutions of representative democracy, the historical legacy of Empire and the cultural sophistication of national collections of art and literature. But this seems somehow bloodless and static, divorced from reality. Where is the best of everyday Australia that many of us value so much: the affability, optimism and sense of possibility?

7.2 During the 1970s Lake Burley Griffin was visited by up to a third of the population on any weekend.

This is the paradox of Canberra and, more specifically, its central institutional space centred on Lake Burley Griffin. While it is meant to represent us Australians, it doesn't do a great job of letting people be a part of what goes on in this area. Watching tourists stagger through the summer heat between the buildings, or the buses disgorging mobs of schoolchildren into the thin shade of the few trees that offer some relief and sense of enclosure, you can see how this bit of Canberra was not a city built for people, but rather a city built for The People—an abstract, undifferentiated populace, most of whom don't have a direct experience of their capital city. And given its (mostly undeserved) reputation as sterile, private and full of public servants and politicians up themselves and out of touch with the 'real Australia', they don't want one. But complicating the ideological landscape, of course, *are* lots of people, and not only bemused visitors. More than 350 000 people live in Canberra, and many of them use these spaces and buildings for work, study and recreation. The sites may be symbolic and national for occasional visitors, but they are quotidian and banal for office workers, runners and cyclists, parents pushing prams, and students.

There are scholarly interpretations of national identity that can help, accounts that treat identity as much more fluid and multiple, a bit more generous to the experience and capacities of the individual. As far back as 1882, for example, French scholar Ernest Renan said that the nation was 'an everyday plebiscite'[4], an entity that people must actively choose to belong to, presumably open to debate and negotiation. Another approach has been to point out that nationalism is made in many different ways, arguing that while nations hold real and deeply felt meaning for people, they are also dynamic, changing and self-reinventing, based on cultures that are 'constantly defined and reconstituted'[5]. Definitions of national identity that emphasise its fluidity and dynamism in this way can be very useful in understanding relatively young, multicultural countries like Australia. But they leave us with the question of how difference is negotiated, how culture is changed. This brings us back to Canberra, which I think is an important location of a process of ongoing re-negotiation of the nation through the frame of its national places.

National identity, national places

I'm not the first person to recognise the importance of the relationship between national identity and national places. The French historian Pierre Nora, in a four-volume analysis translated as 'Rethinking France: *Lieux de Mémoire*', discussed at length the role and meaning of place, among other expressions of culture, in demonstrating the relationship between the national past and the present. Nora reminds us of the importance of what he calls 'vernacular' or popular memory, 'a bond tying us to the eternal present' that never stops working.[6] He saw this as quite distinct from 'official' understandings of history, those that worked from above to shore up particular versions of the nation that were more static and abstract. Nora's notion of '*lieux de mémoire*', or sites of memory (and, by extension, forgetting), are places, texts, rituals and other cultural forms where aspects of national history have been used to reinforce particular ways of understanding the nation itself. In other words, Nora uses history, and its reinterpretation of what is important (and what isn't), to grapple with how national identity is continually being made. Significantly, for the arguments here, he gestures towards place's role as a site of contest between different versions of the nation, speaking to the power of institutions to shape national narratives, as well as the resistance, adherence or even indifference to these narratives by the public. For Nora, history is the storehouse of national content that we can see represented in Canberra's memorials and buildings. But he cleverly activates this history to contemporary social and political ends by dragging it into the present—when these historical representations are evident spatially, the use of these spaces by people helps make and remake them as national. This provides a link between The People and people, through the use and experience of urban places.

There's another important Frenchman to mention here, and that is Henri Lefebvre, who developed the idea of 'the production of space'[7], or that space is an important factor in how social relationships unfold. By emphasising space in this way, Lefebvre drew attention to the ways that power is expressed spatially and the inevitable impact of these expressions, as well as the potential for space to shape both individual identities and human societies. If Nora is focused on the importance of history, Lefebvre reminds us of how all spatial narratives are infused with power relationships. A good example of this process lies in what has *not* been memorialised in Canberra, such as the unsuccessful campaign for an artwork recognising Australian women's suffrage, or the ongoing debate about the design and appropriateness of memorials commemorating Australian involvement in the First and Second World Wars. These examples remind us that national identity, history and power are woven through both what we remember and what we forget.

And this is where Canberra, the symbol, and Canberra, the lived experience, come together uneasily. No one would argue that Canberra's landscape is not a national one. Nor would most people deny the reality

7.3 The Cotter River remains a popular place for families in Canberra.

of its historical representations: from the Griffins' well-known plan, to the monuments that line Anzac Parade, to the buildings themselves, Australia's history is plainly written in the landscape of our capital city. The way this story is represented, furthermore, is controlled, debated and shaped by a select few, not by all Australians. Despite this, the landscape is a personal one, inscribed and remade by the activities of the people who live in it. As monolithic as they are, the national narratives evident in Canberra's layout and design are indisputably complicated and re-narrated by visitors and residents as they use and activate these landscapes. And importantly, these people are not uniform in their use of the landscape, their response to or respect for it, or even their physical engagement. Many, for example, are children, just as Australian as any of us, but with responses to Canberra which might bypass the Grand Narratives and go straight for the personal, embodied and experiential. These Australian people can offer us new ways to read the symbolic landscape, new ways of understanding Canberra's role in the national imagination.

A great place to raise Australian kids

This has certainly been the case for my own children. Despite over a decade living here, we are always leaving Canberra. The departure date is consistently somewhere in the five-year plan, and friends constantly express mock surprise that we're 'still here'. Our children shift nervously when they hear these conversations, because Canberra is, unquestionably, their home. Perhaps I'll never be a Canberran, but they already are. There is no 'real' Australia beyond that of their immediate lived experience, their friends and the environments they inhabit and use.

And why shouldn't this be the case, because one of the things so often said about Canberra is that it is 'a great place to raise kids'. A well-practised list tells some of the reasons: twenty-minute commutes; good public schools; plenty of professional jobs with flexible working hours; safe, well-groomed public parks; no traffic. Of course, this is maddening for people who live in Canberra and don't have children. Even though I am a parent, I can sympathise with frustrations caused by co-workers who leave promptly at 2.30 pm for school pick-up, the impracticality of not being able to start meetings before 9.30 am, and the breezy use of carers' leave to nurse childhood infections that sound vividly Dickensian and contagious. Whether or not you think a place is 'good' for anything varies according to what you value. Small children may love the many local playgrounds and friends within walking distance, but the despondent slouch of teenagers who inhabit those same playgrounds around dusk hints at unspeakable boredom compounded by limited mobility.

Beyond the smug lifestyle factors, there is another way to understand Canberra's contribution to the raising of children, and that is to insert the adjective 'Australian'. When my children were babies, I watched them engaging with Canberra's places, from the local shopping centre to the big national institutions. On one of these occasions, struggling with a pram in the National Gallery, it occurred to me that this national institution might not necessarily consider children as its main audience. This was a shocking insight for someone whose life necessarily, if somewhat tediously, orbited around the demands of very small children. Through a haze of sleep deprivation, it slowly began to occur to me how children's experiences of the city's public places did not necessarily conform to the intentions of the people who designed or maintained those spaces. The smooth pavers of the Sculpture Garden at the National Gallery turned out to be the perfect place to practice bike skills—riding past Rodin, how Canberra! What were they learning about art, culture or identity in such a space? 'Probably nothing', I thought to myself, scraping idly at a mysterious stain on my jumper. But this wasn't entirely true, as they were, of course, creating their own narratives about these places. This included embedding them in our own particular family geography—the fascinating beds of small grey rocks outside the Portrait Gallery, the dangerous hill and spooky tunnel in the garden of the National Museum, the alluring, colourful and irresistibly sharp stained glass in the National Library.

Prominent geographer Doreen Massey[8] writes about how users of place engage in a progressive process that opens space up by linking it to other times and places. Place isn't just what you experience in the here and now, but represents a set of connections to other people in the past and future, and other places that contribute to a site's significance. This approach necessarily emphasises the importance of relationships, and Massey argues that place is always constituted in relation to people, their activities and practices. The everyday activities of shopping, playing, walking and chasing toddlers are examples of such practices, the quotidian just as important as the spectacular.

And this is the crux of my argument: that, by using the ostensibly national places of official Canberra, my children were not only producing their own spatial memories, but were reproducing the places themselves. Perhaps not violently or permanently, gentle vandalism notwithstanding, but through a subtle process of weaving their own experiences into the accumulated histories of these places. Even though they were embedded in the memories of only a few people, when my children and I come to think about where they grew up, our stories will be framed by national symbols that we *know* are national, that are defined by the fact of their national significance. Of course, you could make a similar argument about the role of the beach or the footy field—iconic Australian places if ever there were any, and certainly prominent in many family histories. But such places are not wholly defined by their national roles. The National Library of Australia, the National Gallery of Australia, the National Museum of Australia, all are indisputably and exclusively national. And these are some of the places in which the raising of Australian children occurs.

Of course, these national institutions draw other kids as well, not just those who live in Canberra. Schoolchildren from all over the country come here to learn something about their country and their relationship with it, and they also shape the city in their own ways. Australian schools can apply for a small subsidy to support a visit to Canberra—but they are only eligible if they book to visit Parliament House, the Australian War Memorial, and Old Parliament House and/or the Electoral Education Centre. The powerful narratives that drive the creation of these sites also help shape how, and by whom, they are experienced.

Mostly Year 5/6 students, the largest proportion of children come from Sydney, only a three-hour drive away, and teachers can get official support in organising excursions, accommodation and transport. Canberra's institutions see these children as a core audience, and the visits are popular. In 2010, for example, the Australian War Memorial welcomed 126 000 schoolchildren visitors, a number which had been increasing steadily over the past ten years. Many of these children come back to the Memorial within a couple of years on a family holiday, bringing parents and siblings, thus inscribing Canberra's spaces onto their own family histories. This is important because it suggests that one of the main ways that many Australian families outside Canberra form a firsthand impression of the capital is through the experiences of their ten-year-old children. This begs the question of whether this is preferable to the impression they might form from observing the antics of federal politicians. Childish behaviour aside, this tells us that children matter quite a lot in shaping how the Canberra brand is understood outside the capital. And this clout is likely to increase, as many school excursions to Canberra are linked to civics and citizenship components of the school curriculum, which is currently being standardised across Australia. So what implications might this have for the nation? In many cases, our children are, in effect, narrating the national capital, and the official stories of what 'Australian' is, to their families and friends outside Canberra. Not only is Canberra a great place to bring up kids, it is also a place where Australian kids help build the nation, through their imaginations, experiences, stories, and relationships.

This brings me full circle, back to those first days in Canberra when I couldn't seem to understand what Canberra was *about*. For me, Canberra has always been a gap between the plan and the reality, the official and the vernacular, The People and 'where are all the people'. But in the space between these ideas lies fascinating intellectual territory, which it took the experience of having children—not a pursuit traditionally treated with the greatest intellectual respect—to recognise. Children's use of Canberra manages to unselfconsciously combine the national and the personal, their use of Canberra's symbolic landscape complicating it just a little bit. They blur the official narratives around the edges; they use these places to make their own stories, their own national identities, and their efforts shape Canberra for us all.

Notes

1 Benedict Anderson, 1991 [1983]. *Imagined Communities*, Verso, London.
2 Helen Ting, 'Social Construction of Nations: A Theoretical Exploration', *Nationalism and Ethnic Politics*, vol. 14, no. 3, 2008, pp. 457–8.
3 Eric Hobsbawm and Terence Ranger, 1983. *The Invention of Tradition*, Cambridge University Press, Cambridge.
4 Ernest Renan 'Qu'est-ce qu'une nation?' in John Hutchinson and Anthony Smith, (eds) 1994. *Nationalism*, Oxford University Press, Oxford, p. 17.
5 Umut Özkırımlı, 2005. *Contemporary Debates on Nationalism: A Critical Engagement*, Palgrave Macmillan, Basingstoke, p. 170.
6 Pierre Nora 'Between Memory and History: *Les Lieux de Mémoire*', *Representations*, vol. 26, Spring 1989, pp. 7–24.
7 Henri Lefebvre, 1991. *The Production of Space*, Blackwell, Oxford.
8 Doreen Massey, 'Places and their Pasts', *History Workshop Journal*, no. 39, Spring 1995, pp. 182–92.

8

CULTURAL CAPITAL

David Nichols

Fertile soil

In 1930, an uncredited writer for the Telopea Park Intermediate High School journal *Telopea* observed that, since 'the chief value of History lies in how much we can see of the future in the past,' it was of value to observe—as an object lesson—'that from the earliest times Canberra seems to have been destined as a city of learning and culture.'[1]

There are numerous facets of Canberra's cultural pursuits as the capital—like the nation which has long looked to it with a mixture of fondness and incredulity—'came of age' in its first fifty years. The slow and halting growth of the city, the changing (but usually if nothing else patrician) power structure of its administration, and the particular qualities of its inhabitants give its engagement with, definitions of, and uses of culture a particular importance in Australia. The ways in which it developed a set of cultural expectations and values in the formative decades prior to the Whitlam years throw up fascinating and intriguing manifestations of cultural values—not to mention numerous 'unsung heroes' of Canberra's culture.

Canberra undoubtedly has a special status within Australia. A hundred years on from its initial conception, the city's population is better educated, wealthier, safer and younger than any other of the nation's large cities. Whether it exemplifies the principles intended by the Walter and Marion Griffins and some of their (largely contrary) successors in the city's early decades—honour for the natural landscape, the spiritual and intellectual heart of the nation, a beacon for democracy—is a matter for the beholder. Yet the city withstands all (clichéd) derision from within and without, with calm fortitude. If its citizens were inclined to be drawn into an argument—among themselves, or with the outside world—over the relative advantages of a planned city over an 'organic' one, or the extent to which their social intercourse was managed by their spatial environment or by their government(s), they would nonetheless be compelled to admit that such a discussion was uniquely Canberran.

It could not easily be claimed that the lives, decisions and preferences of Canberra residents impacted on the rest of the nation, and nor could it be said—for the reasons mentioned above, and more—that Canberra has been *representative* of Australia. But at the same time, tracking the cultural life of Canberra since its foundation undoubtedly does provide insight into the nation as a whole. Canberra has often been aspirational, experimental and predictive: journalist Barney Porter's musing in 1939 about a local hope that 'Canberra will be the cultural centre of the Commonwealth' was prescient. Its status as locus for so many important exhibitions, as well as of its own locally derived festivals such as Floriade, shows that this has been partially realised. Remarkable local resources such as the National Museum and the National Gallery of Australia also highlight the jewels of its own residents' endeavours. Additionally, as it builds and explores its own cultural preferences and forays, Canberra has often described an ideal. Just as Canberra's status as a bush capital—that is, an inland city devoted to politics and removed from trivialities of commerce and agriculture which plague other parts of the nation—was an expression of hope for the future of the nation, its consumption and production of culture has made a particularly telling vein of artistic expression.

It is clear from the Federal Capital Commission (FCC)-funded periodical of the mid-1920s, *Canberra Community News,* that the assumption of government and locals was that the new city would develop on modular lines. The paper reported on activities of what were essentially, though not formally identified as, progress associations dedicated to nurturing local community spirit in each of the patchy segments of what was to become the city. These were family-oriented and middle-class associations; single men and women may have been more likely to do their socialising outside the 'dry' capital (between 1910 and 1927) with the notorious weekend exodus to Queanbeyan, known locally as 'Quong'.

Charles Daley was a key figure in both the FCC between 1924 and 1930, and the National Capital Planning and Development Committee after 1939, and notably a defender of the Griffin plan during much of that time. Indeed, he was chief administrator of the capital when he contributed a two-page piece on 'Education in the Federal Capital Territory' to the same first issue of *Telopea* mentioned above.[2] A quarter of a century later, after which Daley had both lived in and comprehensively helped to shape Canberra for over thirty years, he addressed the Canberra and District Historical Society in August 1956 on the topic of 'Early Cultural Activities in Canberra'. The Society was itself a relatively recent 'cultural activity' that Daley had helped to form; he would shortly become its president.

Daley suggests that the opening of the Hotel Canberra at the end of 1924 'might be regarded as the commencement' of cultural activity in Canberra which at that time was a settlement of 4000. However, he singles out Telopea Park School's first building, constructed in 1923, as another distinctive peg in Canberra's shaping, and the Telopea Park Association as the 'most active' among cultural and social organisations. The erection of a series of halls in the nascent nodes of the capital was lauded by the *Canberra Community News* as the basis for the nurture of local talent:

> *[I]t would not be inopportune to add the hope or rather register the conviction, that at some future time films will be shown that have actually been fabricated among the hills of Canberra. Possibly—probably—some local beauty will yet blossom as a movie star of such amazing magnitude that she will conquer not only Canberra, but the outside world as well. Plays are able to be produced, and it is the intention of local aspirants for theatrical fame to show professional protagonists how the Bard of Avon's more famous productions should be mounted and acted. Some confidently look for the appearance of a Juliet and a Hamlet from among those we know and commonly mix with, whose advent in acting will bring managers from Melbourne with long-term contracts in their pockets.*[3]

According to Daley, the first public dramatic performance in Canberra was at one such venue, Causeway Hall; it was Douglas Murray's *The Man from Toronto,* presented by the Canberra Community

Players (later to rename themselves The Scythians). This production was no doubt pragmatically simple to mount: all three acts take place in a cottage parlour.

As a musician, Daley played a part in organising the city's first performing groups, such as the Stromberra Quintet—comprising residents of Mount Stromlo and Canberra—in 1927. This quintet performed on radio at the Opening of Parliament House; the next day Daley was asked to provide piano for a short recital of (what he was surprised to find quickly became) impromptu performances, broadcast around the world. His bemused irritation that his hard work was dismissed by New York critics as 'evidently . . . gramophone records' still burned when he talked about it thirty years later. Local radio for Canberrans came in 1931, and was soon frequented by luminaries representing the Canberra Society of Arts and Literature—'endeavouring to develop the cultural aspect of the people's life'—and the Canberra Music Society. Canberra's cultural resources tended to develop apace with the larger, older metropolises of the nation.

Schools, activities, cultural pursuits: the example of Telopea Park

While it is a cliché to talk of school as a microcosm of wider society, it is true that there are commonalities between the early schools of Canberra and the emerging city itself. The first issue of *Telopea* remarked that the school's 600 students had been 'gathered from every part of Australia, and some, from overseas. The result was that we were almost strangers, and ignorant of each other's abilities.' The school was to become, like many other educational institutions in the city, a petri dish; as it grew, it fostered further schools such as Canberra High over decades.

During the 1930s and 1940s, Telopea Park High School was undoubtedly inhibited in growth like the rest of the nation's institutions; what little press mention is made of its activities such as a 'bright dance' two weeks before Christmas 1936, or the 'high standard' of the eisteddfod in August 1943[4] fails to address the pressures faced. Similarly, little mention is made of wider community engagement with the school, although its buildings were used for adult education from an early period.

The school's activities can, nonetheless, serve as a gauge for the concerns and aspirations of young Canberrans in the post-war years. In the 1950s and early 1960s, plays performed at Telopea Park show a diversity of interests, tropes and prejudices. Modern classics like *Pygmalion* were produced alongside *A Midsummer Night's Dream*. The school already had a tradition of 'Shakespeare in Jeans' omitting, one student journalist enthused, 'the—to us—unnecessary dialogue and boring speech'[5], presented alongside comedic fare such as *The Crimson Coconut* (Ian Hay Beith's 1913 'Absurdity in One Act', including a criminal called Nitro Gliserinski) and *Thirty Minutes in the Street*, a 'representation of the varied and amusing incidents which occur in a street in the modern suburbia'.

Brief descriptions of these performances appear in the school's revived journal, retitled *Capitol* in 1959, alongside student fiction and poetry revealing the common concerns of youth of the 1950s and 1960s: adults' attitudes to teenagers and the cold war—'an object flashed through space and struck Central Australia. In seconds the world became small fragments of matter flying through space'. Students'

8.1 Students relaxing in the grounds of Narrabundah College, circa 1974.

expressions of disaffected angst were all the more heightened in the late 1960s and early 1970s: Julie Harpley's poem 'Friday Night Shopping' canvasses a 'monotonous babble of voices' and 'tired housewives . . . groping grimly back to their cars' and the narrator's return home past 'dark lawns and hedges/Grim, lonely houses'.

Harpley's demonisation of empty consumerism and gender roles was, of course, typical across the western world at this time. However, others chose to attack the national capital specifically. In 1973, two Telopea Park boys—Richard Johns and John Nicolades—penned an extensive critique in which they posited the city as an inevitably redundant consequence of Walter Burley Griffin's political and symbolic affiliations. They wrote of Griffin's plans as having 'created a community, a society, a city in which the lot of the inhabitants has been retrograded by social inadequacies and mistakes,' and continue:

> *The pressures of life in the national capital, civic, political and social, are obvious. Perhaps an indication of the extent to which these pressures apply is the fact that Canberra's suicide rate has been, in recent years, among Australia's highest.*
>
> *There are problems of urbanisation, its associated component of isolation; function, and its pressures; inhabitants, and their needs. It can be summed up by saying that people come to Canberra, but they do not become Canberra.*[6]

The cultural clubs

Johns and Nicolades' disappointment in Canberra's possibilities were hardly unique or new at the time, and nor were they the last to make such complaints. But there were many with greater volition who were able to proactively approach the perceived problem of Canberra's 'social inadequacies'.

The ranks of Canberra's 'cultural clubs' had expanded extensively in the 1950s as the city itself grew. They included the Canberra Film Centre, of which more below, and many were at this time housed in what were known as the Riverside Huts, on land which was soon to be flooded by Lake Burley Griffin.

In 1960, a Cultural Clubs Working Committee was formed by twenty-one societies, including the Photographic Society, the Artists' Society, the Recorded Music Society, Sociedad Hispanoamericana, the Canberra Fellowship of Australian Writers, the Film Centre, Philatelic Society, and the Canberra and District Historical Society. The Canberra Art Club instituted the Committee. All had 'one basic objective' according to an early pronouncement in its working papers 'to find premises in which they can function more efficiently and which will enable them to make a more effective contribution towards the cultural life of this city'. Bringing the cultural societies together in one place was considered imperative for cultural cross-fertilisation and the resilience of culture in Canberra itself:

> *We are strongly of the opinion that this Cultural Centre for Canberra should not simply be a 'dead' display of Australiana but a live, virile, working centre for artists, musicians and others which can, by virtue of its close association of clubs and its physical location, have the maximum impact upon the community and upon each other. Decentralisation of the various clubs would greatly reduce this impact.*

It was also seen by committee members as important for the nation:

> *The cultural clubs in the nation's capital have a greater responsibility in developing and exhibiting the culture of Australia than in any other Australian city. To carry out this responsibility it is essential to have club buildings which are readily available to residents and tourists alike.*

The requirements of the new centre were a familiar 'wish list' with connections to the post-war community centre, and extensive calibrations were made of the ideal room sizes and facilities required; a cinema, offices, meeting rooms and studios were all essential. One studio 'would need good natural light and it would be desirable for it to open out on to a paved, covered outside area which could be used as an outdoor studio'. A small tiered auditorium was needed 'to seat 4–500 people' for the 'Orchestral Society, Repertory, New Education Fellowship and Film Centre.' A quiet 'eating room with a "club" atmosphere where people of like mind could converse over a drink, coffee or a meal' was also posited.

Funding was slowly forthcoming and the new centre was given a site with a proximity to the central city that would surely have been the envy of many similar bodies. Names considered included the Winston Churchill Centre, 'Community Centre', and the Canberry Centre ('reviving an old name for the district'). The name of the 'Griffin Centre' was adopted in May 1965 (the 'Gryphon Centre' was another suggestion; the pun remained in the creature used as the centre's logo). The first stage of the Centre in Bunda Street was opened in 1966. 'Stage 2', it was resolved, 'will include a rehearsal room, a studio and storage'. A draft speech to be read at the opening of the first stage, uncredited in the ACT Council of Cultural Societies, included the following resolution:

> *If Canberra is to take its place as a major capital, it must develop its own especial atmosphere, its own patina of human experience. Unusual and bold ventures like the Griffin Centre, which arise from local needs*

> *and are brought into existence through the initiative of Canberra people, must contribute to this development.*

The second stage of the building, opened in 1969, evinced commentary from Lady Hasluck in her opening speech, which suggests that the centre itself was inspiring Canberrans to new expressive heights:

> *I did not know that there was such a body as The Canberra Toastmistress Club until I saw it in your list. As they practice, do they down the flowing bowl, I wonder. The Australian Tape Recordists' Association was another one new to me, for the very moderns. There are indeed, I can see, many many spheres of amateur interest, as well as the usual artistic ones, which this Centre advances and aids.*

8.2 The Canberra Theatre was opened in 1965.

Special-interest cultural groups in the 1960s and 1970s

Two Canberra clubs stand out as unusual and revelatory of Canberra culture in the 1960s and 1970s: the Canberra Film Centre and the Canberra Science Fiction Society. The National Library of Australia has extensive holdings of newsletters and other materials from both these bodies. Only the former made substantial impact on Canberra that is still visible today.

The Canberra Film Centre was formed in 1944, with the stated intention of promoting 'high standard, informative, educational and cultural films' in the capital (two decades later its *Bulletin* was to describe its initial intention to transcend the 'mere film society showing esoteric films to an esoteric minority'). The centre's formation was tabled at a meeting held at the Institute of Anatomy, where the National Film and Sound Archive is housed today. Its purpose was to borrow educative or other informative films through official channels (such as 'Legations and High Commissioners' Offices')—avenues unlikely to be open to those in other Australian cities.

By the late 1950s, the centre (its aspirational name was never applied to actual premises: the Taglietti-designed Cinema Centre, which opened in Garema Place in 1966, was not directly connected) was holding events such as the Canberra Film Festival, which in 1959 took place in the Albert Hall between 19 and 24 June. The program included films from Spain, Denmark, USSR, Poland, Hungary and Japan. Featured films also included *Pepote (Mio Tio Jacinto)*, *Day of Wrath*, *The House I Live in*, *No Place for Eve to Sleep*, *Ivan the Terrible*, *At Midnight*, *Throne of Blood* and *Fincho*.

It is plain that the centre's organisers were passionate and committed; many also had agendas, both in terms of the prescriptive tone taken in the programs offered, and in the degree to which the centre's presentations were to be educational. Documentary programs, for instance, might include films on Rembrandt, van Gogh, Henry Moore, Graham Sutherland or *Australian Landscape Painters.* Australian film was also often promoted, from the limited material available; a 'Classical Programme' of three Australian short films screened in 1964 included Tim Burstall's five-minute *The Ballad of Ned Kelly,* comprising images of Sidney Nolan paintings, and *Back of Beyond,* a 1953 'impression of life in the inland—along with the infamous Birdsville Track'. The following year, a free screening took place of six short films ranging from 1913 to 1963, all of which featured Canberra itself.

In 1966, the centre announced its intention to present an extensive program of Australian films 'to suggest something of the variety and quality of Australian film production of the past and recent past, to indicate some of the preoccupations of Australian film-makers and sponsors, and to raise questions about the past, present and future of film-making in Australia'. If this did take place, however, it was not covered in later periodicals.

Curiously, when film-making began to take place in and near Canberra itself—for instance, Tony Richardson's *Ned Kelly* (1970) made in Braidwood, and the peculiar political drama *Demonstrator* (1971) filmed in the capital—the presence of very local film-making went unremarked in the centre's *Bulletin.* In the years prior to this, however, it should be noted that local, if amateur, film-making in Canberra had received a boost through the Canberra Cine Club, the formation of which had been sponsored in part by the Canberra Film Centre and promoted in its *Bulletin*.

The channels through which Canberrans might follow their passions and pleasures were varied. One nascent form, which has come to be very familiar in the twenty-first century (and which has arguably morphed in the twenty-first century into the ubiquitous blog), is that of the fanzine. The Canberra Science Fiction Society (CSFS) was founded in 1971, and affiliated with the Cultural Societies at the Griffin Centre, where the Society met on a monthly basis, as a literary group. The CSFS's fanzine, *Nini Hii?* (also often titled *Canberra's Nini Hii?* and, in its earliest form, not titled at all) was edited and published by Helen Hyde in the early 1970s. Hyde used the fanzine—in this case, an irregular photocopied publication of twelve or so pages—to freely discuss not only science fiction texts (in fact, science fiction is often barely mentioned) but also to muse on Canberra itself and its club's members and happenings.

Hyde, formerly a Melburnian and the mother of young children, had no qualms about mixing domestic, observational and 'official' accounts in *Nini Hii?,* creating not only a broad, diaristic view of Canberra life, but also of a small group of enthusiasts and their place in the wider culture—in this case, the budding science fiction scene in Australia. In the second issue, Hyde reflects on Canberra's facilities, planning and recreational opportunities and concludes, 'You will never appreciate a city by sitting and saying "I hate it"'. Issue 8 devoted three pages to a 1925 report on the state of Canberra; another issue included an article on teaching. That said, many of the activities reported on in the fanzine are of trips to Sydney for other conventions or 'minicons'.

This text-heavy, cosy and inclusive publication may be an example of the last gasp of the unassuming, unselfconscious Canberran culture.

A broadening of focus and newly established facilities in the 1970s included the establishment of Australia's third oldest community broadcaster, 2XX, in 1976 and the creation of Bruce Stadium the following year. Not only were these signs that Robert Menzies' recognition of the value of finishing and consolidating the national capital were finding acknowledgement; they were also indications that Canberra was itself achieving critical mass. Perhaps the best examples of this are Canberra's contribution to music in the late 1970s and early 1980s: the Canberra groups Young Docteurs, Tactics, The Church and The Lighthouse Keepers. These bands are today lauded, to varying degrees and in different quarters, as innovators in independent music. It was groups such as these, whose members' talents and skills were nurtured on the stages of Canberra's varied cultural spaces, that achieved the *Canberra Community News*' ambitions a half-century before of attracting 'managers from Melbourne' (or, at least, other larger cities) 'with long-term contracts in their pockets'.

Canberra is an anomaly among Australia's major cities. Comprehensively planned and administered, it remains a model other cities in the nation have for the most part eschewed—to their detriment. Yet this fact is only peripherally relevant to Canberra's *cultural* development. The city's purpose has flavoured the interests and pursuits of its residents: its culture has reflected a motivated, intellectually fertile and purposeful population. As per the nation as a whole, the city has evolved from a performative celebration of western culture (eisteddfods and 'Shakespeare in Jeans') to a stellar contributor to the nation's own cultural production, be it in the music of Tactics' David Studdert, The

Church's Steve Kilbey or the polybanded Nic Dalton, in the writing of Alan Gould or Marion Halligan, or in the thousands of remarkable and valuable exponents, distributors, exhibitors and creators of the arts in the nation's capital.

In 1979 (or thereabouts), Paul Hayward, guitarist with the Young Docteurs, broke a string while performing in Civic. The band filled

8.3 The Canberra Day festival and street parade was a popular event sponsored by the National Capital Development Commission.

a gap with a spontaneous song about, and named for, the street in which they were playing. 'Down in Garema Place,' it went, 'I get my inspiration.' It is typical of Canberrans to both deride and celebrate their city, and to always acknowledge—as so many Australians do—that their circumstances allow them the freedom to be simultaneously dismissive of their unique urban environment as they are nurtured by it.

Acknowledgements

Thanks to Sadie Grant Butler, Gavin Butler, Jane Grant, Nic Dalton, Stephen O'Neil and Tim Ferguson.

Notes

1 C.S. Daley, 'A History of Education in the Federal Capital', *Telopea*, no. 1, 1930, p. 5.
2 'A History of Education in the Federal Capital Territory', pp. 6–7.
3 'C.E.P.', 'The New Halls', *Canberra Community News*, 11 November 1925, pp. 3–4.
4 *Canberra Times*, 19 August 1943, p. 3.
5 R. King, 'Shakespeare in Jeans', *Capitol*, no. 1, 1959, p. 20.
6 Richard Johns and John Nicolades, 'Canberra: Human Dilemma?' *Telopea Park High School*, 1973, pp. 22–3.

9

BELCONNEN MALL

P. Harness

If I could be someone else for just one day
I wouldn't be Prince or Madonna, no way
I would not be the Queen or the King of Bengal
I want to be Belconnen Mall.

Some people think I'm sick, they think I'm over-fixated
When I tell them that I dream of being reincarnated
As a perspex information board stuck on the wall
Of Level 1, Belconnen Mall.

I'm sick of being treated like a second-class citizen
Always getting stuck in the subdivision
I wanna be the focus of people's attention
I wanna be as big as Belconnen Mall.

Well, I try to be polite and have a charismatic presence
Instead I end up feeling like a general nuisance

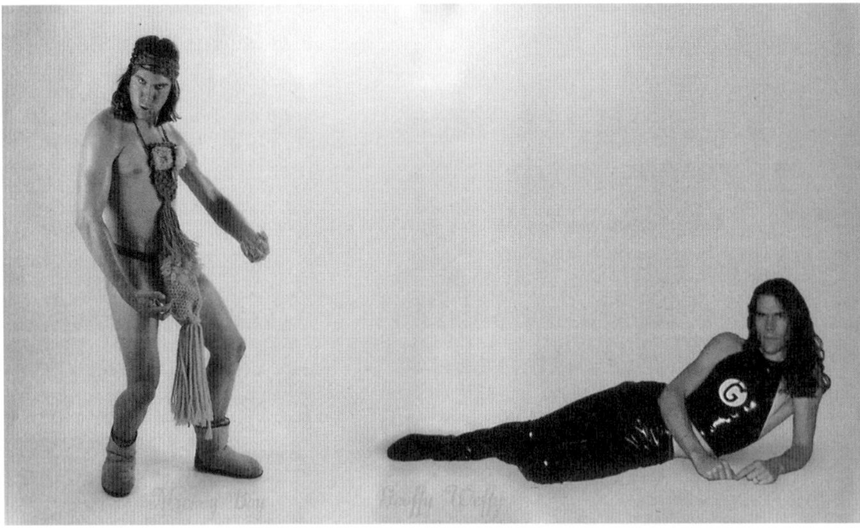

9.1 P. Harness were renowned for their wild stage costumes and antics.

I wanna be desired for public convenience
I wanna be as big as Belconnen Mall.

(Shoppers, we have a lost child with us at the information desk. He answers to the name of Derek and he's wearing some green terry-towelling tracksuit pants and an Iron Maiden t-shirt. Now Derek's cold sores need urgent attention and so does his nappy, and as a special offer today, shoppers, the first lady to claim Derek as her own will receive a free cut 'n' blow from Second Wave on Level 3. Thank you, shoppers.)

I want shops and banks and specialty stores
Like Tandy and Fosseys and Bernina Sewing Centre
I want lifts, escalators, elevators and more
I wanna be as big as Belconnen Mall.

Well, I wanna wear the fashion garments of today
Pastels like pink and purple and beige
I wanna be as spunky as a Sportsgirl display
I wanna be as big as Belconnen Mall.

(Thank you for shopping at Belconnen Mall.)

10

WHEN OUR ETHOS SINGS

Glenda Cloughley

In the half-century since Tom Bass began to body forth the spirit of the Canberra community, Australians have started acknowledging the role of elders along with the traditional custodians of a place and its people. 'Elder' is a term of respect among Ngunnawal and other Aboriginal peoples for wise leaders who carry responsibilities for history, knowledge and guidance on cultural matters.[1] Here, as in other ancient cultures, the elders traditionally pass on knowledge about the laws governing a community through stories, songs, dances, sculpture, paintings and other graphic and ceremonial arts.

Whatever our cultural affiliations, it's a blessing to know a good elder, which is who my friend Tom Bass was to me and perhaps to you, too. Tom touched thousands—maybe millions—of people through his lifework of six decades as a public sculptor and teacher of sculpture. 'No artist has done more to shape the public face of art in Australia than Tom Bass,' John McDonald, art critic for the *Sydney Morning Herald*, wrote during the 2006 Sydney Celebrates the Sculpture of Tom Bass retrospective exhibition at the Opera House. The University of Sydney recognised Tom as Australia's pre-eminent living sculptor with an Honorary Doctorate of Visual Arts in 2009. At his funeral in February 2010, Tim Bass said that his father's lifework was 'a catalyst for something good in our Australian ethos'.

Lineages

Tom was committed to the conservation and creative aspects of his responsibilities as a totemic sculptor. He received and transmitted cultural knowledge in a lineage of teaching artists that he traced through his first teacher Antonio Dattilo-Rubbo to the Italian Renaissance. He also worked hard as a member of another even more ancient and noble—if raggedy and mostly forgotten—European lineage of artists. These are the visionary seers and prophets who listen, like Tom, to 'the great rhythms within', and dreamt something new to meet the spiritual needs of a people in the predicament of a particular time.

The forms these artists produce may shape-shift in response to external changes, but societies depend upon these far-seeing creative people to hear and symbolically represent what's really going on under the hubbub of the market and what the media and government are saying. Carl Jung was thinking of them when he said, 'the artist is constantly at work educating the spirit of the age, conjuring up the forms in which the age is most lacking'.[2] Our present need of them is very great, with international diplomacy faltering and appalling failures of imagination stymying major democracies as climate and other complex planetary systems teeter on catastrophic tipping points. The poignant opportunity still latent in Jung's view that 'art represents a process of self-regulation in the life of nations and epochs' may hang in the balance of social media's global online capacity to circumvent sectional corporate and political interests and reach billions of people with their wisdom.

Tom was related down the European branch of the lineage of seers to the great Athenian dramatist Aeschylus, whose performance record across 2500 years is a kind of longitudinal equivalent to the span of the internet's instantaneous reach. Like Tom, Aeschylus was a superb storyteller. In old age, both these wise men were at the height of their artistic powers and retained a love of conversation, red wine and humour with an unsentimental curiosity about the inner gestures of their own psyches and communities. Both had plumbed spiritual mysteries concerning death and renewal and strove to apply their knowledge to the politics of reconciliation by helping to unfurl the potentials of individuals and communities.[3] Both had strong dreams and occasional visions that shook the core of their beings. They knew myths to be pieces of life, telling the laws that govern what happens.

Though one died in 2010 and the other nearly two-and-a-half millennia ago, they were both concerned that people were out of touch with the laws of nature. In their own ways and with a lot of sorrow, they observed political leaders raising the laws of cities above the laws of nature. Each of these elders devoted himself to doing what he could through his art to turn back the disaster that results from this hubris.

Aeschylus, undoubtedly the darker spirit, was the first writer of Greek tragedy and also contributed substantially to the first democracy. He was a friend, possibly mentor, of the Athenian civic leader Pericles, who sided politically not with the rich and few but the many and poor. His uncompromising use of the theatre to teach the laws of fate through poetry persisted to the closing lines of *The Eumenides*—his final tragedy and the only one with a happy ending—where he amplified the responses to Earth's furious spirits he could hear whispering beneath the community of his city-state into the compelling, healing voices of the civilising divinity Athena and the Citizens' Chorus. As we will see, Tom took a similar line of approach to his most important work in the Australian city-state.

Telos

This brings us to 'telos': a small word from Aeschylus' vocabulary I'd like to introduce you to if you haven't met it yet. Telos means purpose; the condition of maturity, of full development. In philosophy, following Aristotle, it is the final cause.

I am resuscitating this word because it tells us the most significant thing about people—which is who we can be. The telos is what the physicist David Bohm called the 'implicate order'[4] in the cosmos and in ourselves which unfurls itself when the environment permits. The telos is the bright flower in a little brown bulb; the butterfly in a fat cocoon. It is the goal—often, the gift—that draws people along towards the fulfilment of their potential. Telos can be regarded as the destiny of an individual or community spirit; in effect, its destination. Aristotle accorded pivotal status to telos in his book on the nature of politics and cities, which turns upon his beautiful, acutely intelligent observation that *we know a thing by what it has in it to become.* Contemplation of telos is ever-useful in the refreshment of cities as well as psyches, for it is synonymous with the good. Our psychological telos is the energetic force in Jung's observations about individuation, the lifelong process through which we become fully ourselves.

Through temperament and faith, Tom Bass was devoted to the telos in himself, in people he was close to, and in the many Australian communities to which he was deeply connected. The latter includes Canberra's A Chorus of Women, which began on 18 March 2003—as Prime Minister Howard took Australia to war in Iraq—when 150 local women gathered in Parliament House to sing the lament for the people of Iraq that Judith Clingan and I had written four days earlier. Tom recognised that our action became a national media event and the song an anthem for peace, because we had given expression to the voice of Australia that day, which was to sing of the wisdom of peace and grief at its terrible loss.

That Tom was motivated, even compelled, by his telos from the beginning of his work life is clear in this passage from his autobiography, *Totem Maker*: [5]

> *When I finished art school after the Second World War, and was about to embark on my career as a sculptor, I really thought about what sort of sculptor I should be. I looked at the sculpture of all ages and periods, and I tried to find . . . the essential thing about sculpture that made it important at every period.*
>
> *I decided it was this: sculpture is the most social of all the arts.*
>
> *It is something in the open air . . . associated with the great buildings that have a kind of symbolic significance for communities, or with religion . . .*
>
> *Every phase of it that I looked at, I found . . . the sculptor making a significant symbol or totem for the community.*
>
> *The sculptor has always been the seer or spokesperson for the community. I decided that was the kind of sculptor I would become.*

He said this statement was 'the key to who I am'. It is also a key to how he conceived Ethos.

The spirit of Canberra Commission

By 1959, Tom had made several major sculptures for universities, churches and corporations. He called these 'totemic works' because their purpose was to remind people, communities and societies of the things that are most important to them. So he was well chosen by the National Capital Development Commission (NCDC) as the sculptor to represent the spirit of the community of the fledgling city–state of Canberra, Australian Capital Territory.

Tom was thrilled to receive the commission. But soon he was struggling to grasp any symbolic conception for what was brewing beneath this new city that, in 1959, was not much more than a plan for a place of natural beauty and a clutch of ideals about an Australian expression of civilised wisdom, justice and democracy.

Few of the 44 000 people living in the bush capital were born in Canberra, though it was already an interesting place from a multicultural point of view, with many migrants moving there from the Snowy Mountains Scheme to help build the city. There was little suburban development and few national institutions. The Molonglo River hadn't been dammed, so Lake Burley Griffin didn't exist. The Blue Moon Milk Bar was the only café in Civic. Sheep from a local farm often wandered into the grounds of Parliament House.

Prime Minister Robert Menzies was driving development along at a cracking pace after delays resulting from the Great Depression and two world wars. He wanted a sculpture in the City to signify a symbolic municipal centre and so the Canberra Chamber of Commerce—a keen if rather lean force in this government town—became involved with the NCDC in funding the project.

Creating Ethos

Tom was always more intent on public inspiration than material aspiration. So he was not stimulated by the part of his brief urging him to focus on the 'energetic movement of free enterprise'. He was happy enough to focus on the non-political centre of the city, but his imagination refused to follow NCDC and the Chamber into the wild hyperbole of the 'restless and virile' private sector of Canberra in 1959.

'Canberra was not yet really a city,' he wrote in his autobiography. 'It was a synthetic city with a synthetic community.' In 2000, he said, 'I was very aware that these people had not come together out of the dynamic that usually creates a city. They had been roughly torn from all over Australia and sent to Canberra. So they went reluctantly and had no feeling for the place.'

So how did Ethos make herself visible? Much later. Tom thought that perhaps she had really begun in the 1930s when he attended soirées at the Castlecrag home of Walter Burley Griffin and Marion Mahony Griffin. He found Marion charismatic and inspiring, and certainly caught the hope that Walter had expressed in 1912: that Canberra would become 'a city that meets my ideal of the city of the future'.

Tom reflected to me in 2000 that '. . . one day people are going to love this beautiful place. I concentrated on its potentialities and possibilities.' He longed to join the big ideas with his confidence in the power of community in a great symbolic work of art.

Every workday he went to his desk and waited for the right idea to come. As weeks, then months rolled on he fell into a kind of agony. He thought the sculpture would be abstract, but his pen couldn't draw anything that brought the feeling of community spirit and the rational ideas in the city plan together. He produced 'a vast pile of useless drawings'.

Arthur Shakespeare, founder of the *Canberra Times* and a doyen of the Chamber of Commerce, detailed the thing Tom should do: sculpt a figure of a man laying the now iconic Canberra red brick to represent the building of the city. Other people had other opinions, but nothing released Tom from the exacting, awful reality that he had to find the answer in himself.

On Friday, 19 February 1960, Grenfell Ruddock, Chair of the NCDC Co-ordination Committee in Canberra, wrote in his diary about Prime Minister Menzies' visit to the NCDC that day—apparently in a jovial mood. Mr Ruddock noted that the PM . . . has no thoughts of Parliament House being built in his day . . . He is against competitions as a means of selecting architects . . . He is worried about expenditure on the lakes . . . *He wants to see the piece of sculpture . . .'*

Tom told me the other side of this story. When the Prime Minister got someone to ring him and ask where the sculpture was, he had nothing to report. His anguish became nearly unbearable. Finally—desperately—he went to his friend Father Bede, the Franciscan Abbot at the novitiate house in Campbelltown. Tom asked whether the monks would pray for a solution to the problem. The good friar agreed. And the very next morning, in the reverie of sketching, Tom's hand traced the first line of a woman's body.

File notes and other records discovered by Tom's wife Margo Hoekstra and researcher Paul Hendy confirm advice that I often heard Tom repeat: that after inspiration comes a lot of perspiration—including, in this case, of a diplomatic kind. Members of the NCDC Co-ordination Committee were happy with the exquisite maquette Tom presented of a woman reaching up and releasing a dove from her hands. But the National Capital Planning Committee vetoed the dove because it was 'too reminiscent of Picasso'. An ink sketch in which the figure holds up the ACT coat of arms is the next proto-image of the sculpture that has emerged from Tom's files and the city's archives.[6] Finally, late in 1960, the NCDC agreed Tom could proceed after he presented a maquette of the woman reaching to the sun.

The following months were filled with muscular as well as mental feats. He modelled in clay, moulded the clay sculpture in numerous parts and cast copper into the moulds. The copper casts were then welded into the 5.5-metre figure. In the casting, he used the electrolytic copper depositing technique he had pioneered for large sculptural works, which enabled him to cast sculptures before bronze casting was available in Australia.

The name

So there she was, complete in form. But then the fretting returned—this time about the work's name. He thought *The Spirit of Canberra* sounded too much like a train, but nothing else occurred until, one day in the workshop, 'ethos', an unfamiliar word, fell into his mind with the kind of settling clarity that he always respected. If you look up 'ethos' in the *Macquarie Dictionary* you will find it comes into English from Greek, and our word 'ethics' also comes from 'ethos'.

10.1 Tom Bass at work on Ethos in his studio in Minto, New South Wales, 1961.

10.2 Civic Square cloaked in snow with Ethos looking on.

Tom certainly did not know at this time that Aristotle had used the word 'ethos' for the portrayal of character in Greek tragedy, painting and sculpture, and also for the moral competence, expertise and knowledge of a speaker in rhetoric. He wasn't even consciously aware that the word's sociological meaning in English is 'the fundamental spiritual characteristics of a culture'. The Spirit of Community: exactly that.

The way these wise thoughts of artistic intuition and imagination occur is always a mystery. Rationality can't account for them, though they are central in any psychology that includes the telos of the creative human spirit, and usually owe much to the cultivation of states of mind that include prayer, reverie and dream. The fact is that a quality and an image like Ethos is most likely to emerge in someone who has the capacities and generative balance of all true elders: of holding the tension in a community between love and power, relationship and rationality, and of carrying history at the same time as being able to provide guidance for the future.

Other emergent qualities related to ethos and an ethical sensibility which cannot be ordered into existence—even by prime ministers, chambers of commerce and media proprietors—include wisdom, compassion, belonging, peaceful living, goodness, hope, creative living and play, psychological and cultural maturity, the making of meaning and generation of meaningful symbols. In these possible qualities of a city community lies the great telos of democracy that T.S. Eliot pointed to when he said that 'The general ethos of the people they have to govern determines the behaviour of politicians'.[7]

It took Tom so long to see the beautiful face, body and meaning of Ethos because her precise apprehension required *his* passage through a disciplined period of ethical and spiritual preparation in which he went out and met many of the ordinary people of Canberra—curious, engaging, listening to their interests, attachments and hopes in the marvellous way he had. Then he showed up at his desk month after month, and went home knowing the spirit hadn't appeared—that he wasn't ready yet—then recognising her face and form when they did come.

His creative process fully accorded with Professor James Weireck's observation that the strong political views of Walter Burley Griffin and Marion Mahony Griffin arose from their feeling 'that democracy in its essence was about authority coming from within rather than being imposed from without'. The sculpture unites opposite qualities that Tom observed in Marion and Walter, as well as those he came to know in himself. Ethos is, in many ways, a sculptural analogue and personification of the Griffin plan for the ideal city.

In his speech for the unveiling on 15 December 1961, Tom said:

> *The commissioning of Ethos is highly significant. For too long in Australia, communities with very few exceptions have not been prepared to consider anything more in the line of civic art than the local war memorial or stone cairn with a brass plate marking an historic place.*
>
> *Now, from the people of our young National Capital comes the initiative for a piece of civic art to express something more complex.*
>
> *. . . There is, I have found, a strong and very special community spirit emerging in Canberra . . .*
>
> *Nature made Canberra a beautiful place . . . But even apart from its physical beauty there are emerging in Canberra attractive and interesting human attitudes which make the city specially exciting.*
>
> *The people of Canberra are identifying themselves with their city—not in any selfish, self-satisfied parochial sense—but with a sense of belonging to a growing metropolis—already Australia's largest inland city and the centre of a large region.*
>
> *With Ethos I have tried to provide a focal point for the affection the people of Canberra feel for their city.*
>
> *. . . Ethos meets the basic requirements for my conception of what civic art in Australia should try to achieve.*
>
> *Both the artist and the society can benefit from the development of civic arts which aim to serve the community, to enrich the imagination, to clarify and enlarge the sensibilities and the consciousness of the people.*

Our civic art, I believe, should attempt to attain dignity, freshness and conviction to become a genuine expression of the life of the people.

Meeting Ethos

Since 1961, Ethos has stood with quiet grace outside the front entrance of the ACT Legislative Assembly. As the city changes around her, she continues to embody something of Walter Burley Griffin's hope that Civic Square would become the 'living heart' of Canberra.

The substantial ACT Heritage Register citation for Ethos describes the work as 'highly symbolic'. The saucer bears a relief map of Canberra, including the lake that would later lie between the Civic centre and the Parliamentary Triangle. She is humanly proportioned. Her facial expression is serious yet soft. The posture and raised wings suggest civilising, spiritual qualities. The figure is robed in a fabric embossed with images of people and symbols of ancient civilisations. Reaching to the sun, Ethos points to the rational as well as relational basis of governance. The Heritage Register citation quotes Tom's speech for the unveiling: 'The bursting sun she holds aloft is symbolic of culture and enlightenment which the presence of Canberra's university, its research organisations and the Diplomatic Corps and so on give to the city.' If you visit Ethos on a clear summer day, you will see that even her dancing shadow is beautiful.

These qualities are integral to the view of former Chief Minister John Stanhope that Ethos is 'arguably the most significant public artwork in Canberra'. Yet they don't add up to the numinous, steady hope I have felt in her presence and seen manifest on the faces of Canberrans, tourists and many children.

10.3 Ethos at night

The source of this subtle potency is surely the generative capacity of a woman, which the master sculptor at once annunciated and concealed. With ovoid shaping, the strong line encircling her hips, and something ineffable from the spiritual core of himself, Tom made the womb of Ethos the warm, inner centre of the figure's gravity and telos so that, mysteriously and wondrously, while not being obviously pregnant, Ethos is always gestating.

Community focus

Through half our city's century, Ethos has been alive in the people. Her image and name have been claimed to express diverse epiphanies of community spirit—from a young impersonator aboard the 'Kinship' float in an early Canberra Festival Parade to the miniature gold Ethos lapel badges worn by the freemasons of Canberra's Ethos Masonic Lodge; from the Ethos logo with a shimmering treble clef between her arms that Judith Clingan created for the 1971 Ethos Intervarsity Choral Festival to the wild-haired Ethos building logo Canberra Museum and Gallery mounted in 1998; and from the music of Ethos Band's monthly gig at the Hellenic Club in Woden to Elizabeth Cameron Dalman's exquisite performances of 'Ethos Dancing' when Tom spoke to the Jung Societies of Canberra and Sydney in 2001 and 2002.

Tom's delight in the community uptake was thoroughly inclusive. The sculpture's dignified womanliness may be antithetical to the Chamber of Commerce's visions of throbbing virility, yet he was very happy when the Commonwealth Bank named its London Circuit building 'Ethos House'. He loved that Barry Humphries asked a Canberra Theatre audience: 'Who is that woman out there holding up a meringue?'

In 2001, he attended the Canberra Festival Opening Pageant for the second unveiling of Ethos after Artistic Director David Branson had arranged for her wrapping Christo-style in white cloth. I looked nervously at Tom twice that night and discovered him enjoying the show both times—once when a huge and rather hideous Ethos puppet appeared, and again when someone had to abseil down the real Ethos to undo the wrapping after the cherry picker broke. Two years later, when Australia was at war in Iraq, he supported Canberra's Women in Black who covered Ethos in a black shroud throughout their silent vigil in Civic Square.

The voice of Ethos

This final story tells some ways in which Ethos continues revealing her telos to us—and through us. In 2005, when Tom was eighty-nine years old, A Chorus of Women wanted to create a ceremony around Ethos for a Festival of Peace in the ACT Legislative Assembly that was being sponsored by women Members of the Legislative Assembly from all three political parties. The purpose was to celebrate the ninetieth anniversary of the Women's International League for Peace and Freedom—the organisation to which Picasso donated his famous drawing of the dove. I visited Ethos and listened, hoping she might give us a song. Then I had a better idea. I phoned Tom and asked whether he thought Ethos might have something to say to the city after all the years of standing there quietly. 'Mmm, we'll see,' he said in his warm, deep voice. A few mornings later he rang me in great excitement. He had woken at 4.30 am from a dream in which Ethos was speaking to him. We read what she said during a ceremony involving girls and women of all ages:

I am Ethos

though I do not
speak with words
I speak to you
in other ways

I say to you that
I am the spirit
of this place
and its people

I am
the original spirit
and the spirit of now

I rise from the earth
and reach to the sun

I bring together
the old and new

in me there is
no violence or war
only peace
and reconciliation

I am the love
peace and beauty
of this place

I give you
these things
every day
and always

Next time you visit Ethos, you can read the poem again because Tom engraved it in a plaque that has been set into the pavers beside the sculpture.

In May 2009, Tom made another statement about Ethos:

> *As the creator of the sculpture, Ethos, it was my hope that she would inspire the people with the value and importance of community. I expressed this through her brocaded garment, the earth she stands on and the sun that enlightens it.*

At this time, A Chorus of Women was planning a season of a mythic story-song I had composed about relations between people and Earth in the Museum of Australian Democracy at Old Parliament House with a cast of eighty intrepid Canberra citizens. *The Gifts of the Furies* it's called, and in it Ethos takes the role played by the wise, civilising divinity Athena in Aeschylus' *Eumenides,* on which I based the work.

I checked with Tom throughout my process of bringing Ethos to life. You can hear quite a lot in other parts of Tom's statement of support about his original vision of what Ethos would become in the Canberra community. He said that in *The Gifts of the Furies*:

> *Ethos takes full possession of her role as the Spirit of the community. She expresses the yearnings of the time, in which peace and reconciliation are central. She also enacts her role as the intermediary between the forces of earth and heaven. With climate change being the crisis of our times Ethos's actions are those of a loving and wise guide.*[8]

'Dear Marion'

A Canberra Lab project

By Ronan Moss, James Park & Gerard O'Connell

MUSEUM OF AUSTRALIAN DEMOCRACY

OLD PARLIAMENT HOUSE

9 316134 001785

STANDARD POSTAGE

Dear Marion,

Do you remember this day?
Did they invite you?
They have moved on from that
frumpy building and built a
new Parliament. Come and visit!
I will take you on the tour. With love. Walter.

Marion Mahoney
1 Carton Ave
Archi-Heaven
1101-

MUSEUM OF AUSTRALIAN DEMOCRACY KING GEORGE TERRACE PARKES CANBERRA MOADOPH.GOV.AU

MUSEUM
OF AUSTRALIAN
DEMOCRACY
OLD PARLIAMENT HOUSE

9 316134 001785
STANDARD POSTAGE

Dear Marion, I found
this in the gift shop.
Strange nostalgic vision
of times past. Funny
how the city still kind
of looks like this today!
Sans sepia toned sheep of course.

Marion Mahoney

1 Corbu Ave
Archi-Heaven
1101-

With
love
Walter.

MUSEUM OF AUSTRALIAN DEMOCRACY KING GEORGE TERRACE PARKES CANBERRA MOADOPH.GOV.AU

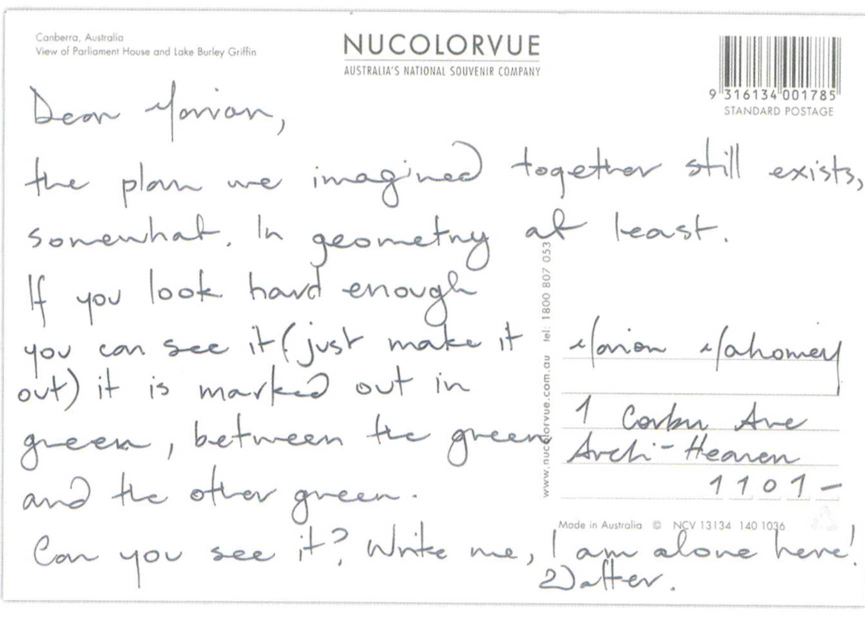

Canberra, Australia
View of Parliament House and Lake Burley Griffin

NUCOLORVUE
AUSTRALIA'S NATIONAL SOUVENIR COMPANY

9 316134 001785
STANDARD POSTAGE

Dear Marion,
the plan we imagined together still exists,
somewhat. In geometry at least.
If you look hard enough
you can see it (just make it
out) it is marked out in
green, between the green
and the other green.
Can you see it? Write me, I am alone here!
Walter.

Marion Mahoney
1 Corbu Ave
Archi-Heaven
1101 –

www.nucolorvue.com.au tel: 1800 807 053

Made in Australia © NCV 13134 140 1036

RENO

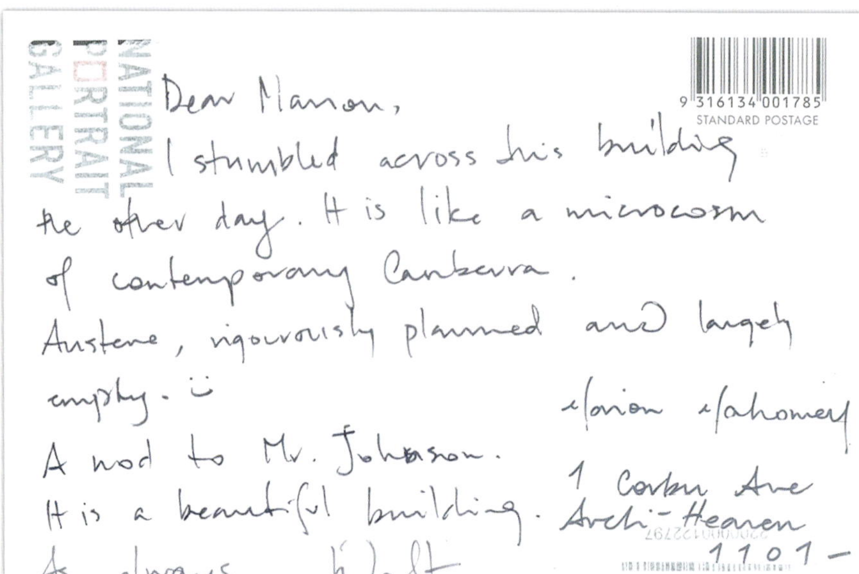

NATIONAL PORTRAIT GALLERY

9 316134 001785
STANDARD POSTAGE

Dear Marion,
I stumbled across this building the other day. It is like a microcosm of contemporary Canberra. Austere, rigourously planned and largely empty. :)
A nod to Mr. Johnson.
It is a beautiful building.
As always, Walt.

Marion Mahoney
1 Corbu Ave
Archi-Heaven
1101 –

CANBERRA AUSTRALIA

Dear Marion,

The lake is just as we imagined it. Perhaps even better... But for all the bold axies and connections to the landscape, the city creeps tentatively, almost fearfully towards the Lake during the day; dips it's toe in the water, shreiks, and flees from it by nightfall. Its a shame.

Marion Mahoney
1 Corbu Ave
Archi-Heaven
1101 —

It would be great to hear from You! Walt.

July 2012. In a moment of clarity, Walter Burley Griffin agrees to return to Canberra. Finding himself alone amidst a strangely foreign landscape, his thoughts turn to the love of his life, and co-creator: his Dear Marion. As Walter slowly rediscovers the nation's capital, he comes to reinterpret and challenge the nature of 'the ideal city'.

The intent of 'Dear Marion' is multi-layered. It tests the notion of the Grand Vision, and offers up myriad potential designs—'little ideals'—resulting in a dense and rich urban fabric. Collage and overlay are critical concepts of 'Dear Marion' and, as such, Walter's proposals naturally occur in the underutilised 'gaps' of the city—verges, alleyways, the tops of buildings.

'Dear Marion' encourages direct engagement with the city and its inhabitants. Walter appears in unexpected locations, sometimes offering critique, other times solutions. Passersby can interact with Walter—'friend' him on Facebook, chat to him on Twitter—and thereby question the assumptions they make about the city and its workings.

www.canberralab.com

For the Old Parliament House performances and others at the Tom Bass Sculpture Studio School in Sydney and elsewhere, we have been loaned the beautiful, portable bronze *Head of Ethos* that Tom sculpted in his ninety-third year just a few months before he died.

A Chorus of Women continues to draw guidance from the image of Ethos in such Civic Square activities as our series of nine *Canberra Conversations* on matters of community significance, and occasional ceremonies like those we organised across the divide of the 2006 war between Israel and Hezbollah so people could come together to break bread, share their grief and sing.

On International Day of Peace in September 2007, we gathered 200 singers from eight choirs around Ethos before setting out on the Chorus of Women—UNIFEM Spring Sing through Civic and the Canberra Centre.

The Chorus moved Tom to tears with the first, surprise performance of the song 'I Am Ethos'—my musical setting of the 'Ethos Speaks' poem—after the screening of the 1968 film about his National Library lintel sculpture which was part of the Library's fortieth birthday celebrations in 2008. Later, I learned that yet another ancient Greek usage of the word 'ethos' was for the power of music to influence hearers' emotions, behaviors, and even morals.[9]

For the fiftieth birthday of Ethos on 15 December 2011, A Chorus of Women organised a celebration in Civic Square and the Legislative Assembly with sponsorship from Chief Minister Katy Gallagher and Members from all parties. This happy event brought Tom's family and friends together with a wide range of community leaders and groups who all walked the meditative path of Alison Meretini's labyrinth around the sculpture and joined in the first community singing of 'I Am Ethos' as an anthem for the city.

In this centenary year, to encourage Canberrans of all musical tastes to make 'I Am Ethos' their own, the Chorus has recorded three infectious arrangements—with community singing by a large group of men and women; the a cappella voices of Judith Clingan, Meg Rigby, Johanna McBride and me; and a folk-rock version created by Jenny Sawer, Nitya Bernard Parker and Andrew Purdam.

This last story ends with a sweet mystery that revealed itself in 2010 a few months after Tom died. I was preparing a paper called *Looking at Ethos* for the Inaugural Conference on Wisdom in Management at the ANU College of Business and Economics. And I was thinking about the unsigned plaque beside Ethos as a specifically Tom-type wise form of faithfulness to dreaming.

Three years before this, when Tom, Margo and I had met with Chief Minister Stanhope and some senior Canberra arts people, the ACT government agreed to pay for the plaster model of the plaque to be cast in bronze. Arts Advisor Penelope Layland said: 'You haven't signed the poem, Tom.' In reply, he said: 'I did not write the poem. Ethos is the author.'

The delicate, respectful silence in the Chief Minister's office that followed his statement is now fixed into the pavers of Civic Square along with the hopeful telos in Tom's comment to me not long before he died—that he was glad that Ethos would still be here when he was gone. And the sweet mystery? It is that although dear, wise Tom Bass has passed away from us, Ethos *is* still here, and she could speak—or even sing—to you too.

I am Ethos

AN ANTHEM FOR THE CANBERRA COMMUNITY

Words spoken by Ethos to her sculptor
Tom Bass in a dream during October 2005

Music Glenda Cloughley

10.4 Manuscript for 'I Am Ethos' by Glenda Cloughley.

Acknowledgements

Special thanks to Margo Hoekstra, Johanna McBride and all the singers of A Chorus of Women and Canberra Citizens' Chorus.

This essay about Tom Bass and his Canberra sculpture Ethos is adapted from the Tom Bass Memorial Address in the Australian Theatre for Young People, Sydney. Also performed on that occasion was *The Gifts of the Furies*, the author's mythic drama about climate change in which Ethos leads the people towards sustaining forms of reconciliation with the fearsome spirits of Earth.

Notes

1 My description of elders is drawn from the Aboriginal and Torres Strait Islander Protocols of the City of Sydney, where I gave the Tom Bass Memorial Address.

2 Carl Jung, 1991. *The Archetypes and the Collective Unconscious*, 2nd edition. Routledge, London.

3 See Clara M. Smertenko, 'The Political Sympathies of Aeschylus', *Journal of Hellenic Studies*, vol. 52, part 2, 1932, pp. 233–5.

4 David Bohm, 1980. *Wholeness and the Implicate Order*, Routledge, London.

5 Tom Bass and Harris Smart, 1996. *Tom Bass: Totem Maker*, Australian Scholarly Publishing, Kew, Victoria.

6 Tom's first wife Lenore Rays was later commissioned to sculpt the large Coat of Arms above the public entrance to the ACT Legislative Assembly.

7 T.S. Eliot, 1940. *The Idea of a Christian Society*, Harcourt, Brace and Company, New York, p. 25.

8 Tom Bass, 2009. Supporting statement to Arts ACT for A Chorus of Women's successful funding application.

9 David Castriota, 1992. In *Myth, Ethos, and Actuality: Official Art in Fifth-Century B.C. Athens* Castriota states that early Greek stories of Orpheus exhibit this idea in a compelling way. University of Wisconsin Press, Madison, WI.

11

MADE IN CANBERRA

Susan Boden and Nicholas Brown

'That was when the world wasn't so big and I could see everywhere.
It was when my father was a hero and not a human.'
Markus Zusak, *The Messenger*

The contribution of Robert Boden (1935–2009) to Canberra's urban treescape has two highpoints: his early work as a young forestry graduate at Yarralumla Nursery (appointed in 1955), and later directorship of the Australian National Botanic Gardens (1979–89). In between were periods of research, work on national and international conservation management and policy, and the establishment of his suburban and rural gardens in partnership with his first wife. He was, at his death, remembered as 'an articulate advocate for a greener Canberra'[1]—and, more familiarly and fondly, by many as the regular presenter of an early local television program offering gardening advice, and later as a columnist on 'favourite trees' and a correspondent for the *Canberra Times*. This is not a biography of his public life through those years, but a place for us—as his daughter (landscape architect) and son-in-law (historian)—to unwind some of our experiences as children in the planned environment he helped to create. Our perspective is informed by Robert's first impressions of Canberra and its possibilities, as he began his participation in shaping what would come to be called its 'urban forest'—the landscape element that, with Lake Burley Griffin, still most evokes the national capital, and gives it coherence.

Planting Canberra's streets

Parents can either give insight through their illuminating vision or create opacity for their children, and sometimes both at once. In this sense, our memories of childhood and the way we understand Canberra now through our educated eyes is a perspective that is both clear in details and outline, yet sometimes blurred in assumptions. Robert's experiences can help us gain a sharper balance between these elements.

We were both born in 1961, two years before Lake Burley Griffin was completed, and four years after the National Capital Development Authority (NCDC) was established to coordinate the development of the city. Our Canberra was assured a future and a form. Its new suburbs were laboratories of integrated neighbourhood planning. No facility (preschool, school, shop or clinic) was to be more than a pram-push distant from private homes. Not only were the streets planted in advance, but a generous allocation of free trees and shrubs was extended to residents to help them settle and shoulder their part in consolidating the city. If nothing else could be said of it, Canberra was for our generation 'a great place for children'.

When Robert arrived in 1954, Canberra still felt tentative. The eminent architect Robin Boyd judged that as a planned city, it reached 'nadir' that year, as moves were made to delete the entire western reach from Griffin's lake scheme or to construct roads that violated his

Parliamentary Triangle. To a visiting American, Canberra seemed then 'a unique little monstrosity'.[2] Mounting concern that the Commonwealth Parliament must either 'assert its position' on the city or 'surrender it' led to the appointment of a Senate Select Committee by November. Its task was to review what its chair, Senator J.A. McCallum, damned as the 'dawdling, doddering manner' of development which had prevailed since 1913, devoid of 'imagination, vision or energy'.[3] The city was in crisis, if in ways that a nineteen-year-old student could scarcely apprehend.

As soon as he arrived, Robert wrote regularly—at least weekly—to the family he had left in Sydney, in part offering assurance of his welfare, in part finding consolation across distance, but mostly with a joy of independent discovery.

Drawing on nine of these letters, we have tried to be truthful to Robert's impressions and ideas through our understanding of him and his context. The significance of these letters, here, is in the extent to which they suggest a synthesis and turning point for a city and a life. We are aware that these were private letters to his parents, aunt and grandmother. Why only nine letters remain is unclear, but the care in their preservation and safekeeping through three generations (Robert's mother, Robert, Robert's daughter, Susan) was deliberate. They anticipate a journey, and highlight choices.

A fully motorised town

For both of us, the 'Canberra' of our childhoods was familiar and ordinary. But at the same time, the vision of its planners (from the Griffins on) would have been a complete failure if their spatial lessons in civics had made no impact on us.

We had no sophisticated concepts to understand large, pale buildings, broad straight roads and oversized, isolated monuments. But we felt their impacts on roundabout bus rides past designed places empty of people. Our Canberra was profoundly shaped by the principles of Sir William Holford, a town planner invited from Britain in 1957 to advise on how the city might be transformed in the light of Senator McCallum's recommendations. He offered the ideal of 'a fully motorised town', to be experienced primarily in the family car, while affirming the 'garden city' model and gesturing more 'awkwardly' to a 'city of culture' which might celebrate Australia's 'surplus wealth'.[4] In 1961, the NCDC commissioned Tom Bass' embodiment of Canberra's 'ethos' as a winged figure, holding aloft the sun and rather primly poised above the small bowl of the city—a message reinforced by the sculpture's placement in neatly paved 'Civic Square'[5]. As Prime Minister in the 1920s, S.M. Bruce had loathed the way in which Griffin's functional descriptor of a zone—'Civic'—at the end of a commercial boulevard had become a place name, leaden in its usage. But for us, 'Civic' was just accepted, even though, in 1963, rather than centring on municipal buildings, the precinct centred on Australia's first fully enclosed, air-conditioned shopping mall.

We knew from trips to Sydney that Canberra was different, and Susan had grandparents who felt it necessary to advocate for the benefits of Canberra when they returned home and talked with their neighbours and friends. We also took note of the large official buildings with crests and flags that took up a lot of space but were only really viewed or visited when interstate visitors came to stay. Mainly, however, we experienced the city as a resolutely modern project, setting standards we assumed others must follow. Our kindergartens were modern, as were our schools, and—when the ACT Schools Authority broke with the services of the NSW Department of Education in 1977—we were the first into the experimental model of a secondary college system premised on 'continuous school-based assessment', no external examination, and a learning style in which we sat on carpets and called teachers by their first names. We had benefited from Prime Minister Menzies' ambition in the 1950s to 'build up Canberra as a capital in the eyes and minds of the Australian people'; we were experiencing Gough Whitlam's desire to use the city to force the pace of change.[6]

'Expectation and aspiration'

Our experience of this rather uncanny Canberra as children was matched by the interests of academic researchers. In 1970, Hugh Stretton vaunted 'the Canberra method' of integrated suburban planning as promising a more 'original and marvellous achievement' than could be hoped for, as was perhaps necessary in, 'the tombstone park' around parliament.[7] Writing in 1975, resident and geographer G.J.R. Linge described an energetic city, populated by 'car-conscious' residents driven by 'expectation and aspiration'. It is a neat fit that Linge wrote this while Professor of Geography at the Australian National University (ANU), itself a beehive of scientific, social science and humanities inquiry. In fact, the founding mission of the ANU in 1946—now rendered as supporting 'the development of national unity and identity . . . and social cohesion'—can be read as a rationale for the post-war city, in which residents enacted a common post-war pattern of distancing themselves from the past and taking advantage of the economic growth that victory, recovery, prosperity and the spill-over of military technology into consumer products allowed.[8]

Like Linge's, our Canberra was 'vigorous, new, clean'. Our parents participated as good citizens across a range of private and public suburban tasks. They joined committees, shaped homes and gardens, thought at least passingly about Cold and Hot Wars but were probably more concerned by managing the capital's seasons, as they shepherded children through school terms and long summer holidays. Our mothers worked especially hard in paid and unpaid roles, with a combination of dedication, diligence and, probably, frustration. Their version of Canberra's now dominant 'café experience' was a thermos and folded picnic rug spread over crazy-paved seat walls provided on the lake shore. Our fathers were also serious about their suburban domestic lives. With pragmatic and sometimes over-reaching plans, they paved patios, mixed pungent garden chemicals and built houses for whichever pet animal was supposed to encourage responsibility in their children (but fell, as another task, to our mothers). Appropriately, when Robert chose a PhD topic in 1968, it was to analyse the ways in which Canberrans used rural, river and forest areas beyond the city for an increasingly variable range of recreational purposes, his argument centring on the challenge of balancing a sense of access and amenity to the costs of management and environmental impact.

Made in Canberra

But for Nicholas there was a longer history in Canberra. Descended on his father's side from a convict labourer indentured to the region in 1835, he still had family on the land near the Cotter River. His mother had moved from Hobart after the war to join the typing pools serving the great expansion of central government, and experienced austere hostel life until she married. His father, returning from war, was an early recruit to the Department of Immigration, one of the few Commonwealth agencies to be established in Canberra during the 1940s, but also one of the clearest signals of a new commitment to nation building. Bill Brown had postings to Athens and Rome in the late 1950s, where his job was to select prospective 'New Australians'. A proud public servant, he exemplified—embodied—the management of policy (in his case, 'White Australia') so as to minimise the public exposure of government, engineering (as he put it) 'gradual amendments, gradual improvements, to condition the Australian people' to any prospect of change.[9] In his later years, it was common for him to be warmly met by grateful immigrant families who had flourished in Canberra, if at first in carefully designated 'worker's suburbs'—and thankfully, only once was he held to account for 'letting me in, but not my brother!'

Susan's parents both came from Sydney. As was a common pattern, the path was forged by Robert, when he arrived to complete his forestry degree at the Australian Forestry School, Yarralumla. In 1927, that school had been one of the earliest national institutions established in the city, reflecting a commitment to a discipline that combined industrial and conservation management, and an ideal of science in the public service that then defined the national capital more effectively than government itself. The school also connected closely with Canberra's Garden City model.[10]

In his training, and after 1955 in his employment, Robert's 'new Australians' were the hundreds of exotic tree species that he planted, along with native trees, in an effort to delineate, humanise and ameliorate a grand national project. This project had a history dating back to the Griffin years, when Thomas Weston, as officer-in-charge of afforestation (1913–26), planted around two million trees with the aim of moderating a harsh climate and repairing a denuded pastoral landscape. In keeping with this tradition, much of Robert's work was experimental. He was wise enough to recognise the ultimate primacy of environmental factors in acknowledging, towards the end of his life, that 'the best trees I ever planted were probably the ones that didn't survive'.

Born in 1935 in Sydney, the younger son of draftsman Gordon and homemaker Jean, Robert had a childhood that was comfortable and secured by local cousins, aunts and uncles and, on his father's side, a family from west-coast 'Tassie'. A stern maternal grandmother and the intrigue of a grandfather who had been lost along the way in country New South Wales capped his extended family. Both Robert's parents were skilled with their hands and temperamentally shaped by the economy of Methodism. The stringency of the economic Depression of the 1930s and, in his mother's case, the experience of 'reduced circumstances' following the separation of her parents, encouraged economy—sometimes unnecessary—in them both. Gordon and Jean led parallel lives but with the common aim of producing a 'good' family. When their lives overlapped, they took up defined roles. The toaster, screwdriver, Christmas wrapping and washing up were Gordon's 'inside' activities. Jean kept well clear of the workshop and garage except to get her shopping trolley or gardening hat. But the place where their lives and roles were shared was their suburban Earlwood garden.

Robert's arrival in Canberra was, in some ways, accidental. He had wanted to be a vet, but his parents were not prepared to finance a university education. A Commonwealth Forestry Scholarship made study possible. After beginning his studies at the University of Sydney, he transferred to the Australian Forestry School—itself emerging from its own sometimes tortuous path of asserting a national authority, consolidating a determined professionalism among graduates, and adapting a discipline once conceived in strongly Imperial terms to a role in the emerging 'green revolution' of technical assistance to 'developing' countries. As much as Canberra was at a nadir, it still offered a microcosm of all that these elements represented—and in ways that infused not only Robert's context and opportunities, but also his experience and professional temperament.

'Simply perfect'

Robert searched throughout his working life for a word to describe both his forestry practice and empathy with trees. Although he worked with shrubs and in later research with the modified grassland agricultural landscapes on Canberra's edges, his loyalty was to plants 'taller than me'. Robert liked 'arborist' but 'urban forester' is probably the more accurate description, with the understanding that forests, like human communities, were, for him, aggregates of widely differing individuals. Robert's 'urban forests' were built in his mind and physically, through his planting, tree by tree. As a father, and quietly, Robert would show his children trees that he had planted—including, ironically, the street tree species that had survived more as a horticultural experiment than a successful scheme.

When Robert came to Canberra, Lindsay Pryor—a successor to Weston—was well advanced in introducing a more informal style into Canberra's treescape, trialling hybrid species on site as well as in nurseries, and with a particular interest in eucalypts. Canberra might have been easily ridiculed (as Kylie Tennant put it in 1945) as a 'landscape . . . carefully planned not for the convenience of human beings but of trees', but equally, into the 1950s, it was the trees that seemed its one salvation.[11] McCallum's committee enthusiastically endorsed Pryor's argument that a twenty-year forward program was required to provide an infrastructure of 'parks and gardens' into which the city could grow. It gave 'unstinted praise' to those charged with this work, lamenting only an official disposition to use trees in the city to 'hide ugliness' rather than 'enhance and create beauty'.[12] In this context, Robert's work would flourish—but it could not be taken for granted.

By 1954, Canberra's population had grown over five years from just over 19 000 to over 30 000; and in housing, let alone offices or community facilities, the city was falling further behind in providing for the new inhabitants. The Petrov defection, on the eve of the May 1954 federal election, brought the Cold War into its leafy precincts, and severely affected what had seemed to be the Labor Party's prospects of victory. Had H.V. Evatt ousted Menzies, the victory for progressive politics might have been significant, but with what impact on the growth of Canberra that Menzies soon championed? And, even as McCallum's Committee endorsed—once again—the primacy of the Griffin plan, it was the case that the plan was esteemed by them more for its 'pastoral' than urban elements. There existed at that point only the faintest traces of the formal arrangements of the original Griffin plan, often in forms marked out by Weston's planting, and vulnerable to the 'frankly picturesque' and suburban-oriented preferences that would follow from Holford. Robert—like many at the time—exercised a fair degree of intuition in discovering and making the capital, and in conveying its distinctive character.

11.1 Robert Boden (under telegraph pole) with fellow Australian Forestry students, Canberra region, 1954.

He had not yet read accounts by early Europeans who made sense of the east coast Australian landscape by seeing it in terms of an open, pleasant parkland. But by taste and experience, his default was the same, and the informality of the city mattered more than its formality. He wrote, tongue in cheek, of

> *. . . visiting the Governor General today but we were stopped at the front gates. The house itself looks towards the west and the pine covered hills. From the main road there is a drive passing through beautiful parkland . . . The trees are lovely.* (13 March 1954)

After he bought a bike for six shillings—and then learned to ride it—he hoped to '. . . be able to see a lot more of the beauty of Canberra. It is beautiful just riding slowly along the avenues of trees whose branches almost form an archway' (4 April 1954). Noting that the city was full of 'kookaburras and an occasional rabbit' (undated), Canberra was largely a benign place, although Robert wrote with relief that

> *. . . I have so far avoided National Service and hope to continue doing so. I am sure the work here is of greater constructive importance to Australia's benefit than learning how to kill people.* (4 April 1954)

As a student forester, Canberra's climate and weather interested Robert and made a strong point of connection with his mother who had also grown up with crisp mornings and bright night skies on the NSW Central Tablelands. He wrote that Canberra's late March weather was '. . . simply perfect' (28 March 1954), and was relieved that 'there is none of Sydney's dreadful humidity' (28 March 1954). Instead 'a lot of the oaks are just changing colour and they seem to go straight to a reddish colour and there is little of the yellow of the poplars' (4 April 1954).

By winter, the weather was the coldest he had experienced. Unlike many past and current critics of Canberra's cold, Robert loved it:

> *We have had some very heavy frosts this week the lowest temperature being 19° F which is 11.4° F of frost as the grass temp for a frost is 30.4° F. The oval looks really beautiful in the mornings as the frosty mornings are usually very clean and everything sparkles. I quite like the crisp sharp cold.* (19 June 1954)

Throughout the winter, fieldwork continued including mass tree planting in a remote commercial pine plantation. Despite the cold and winds, Robert saw something beautiful in the punctuated days and seasons that Sydney's humid, temperate climate lacked:

> *It is a beautiful clear night with the stars sharply defined. The country nights have a clearness and beauty so different from the city nights as you no doubt know after living at Narromine. Coming across the oval was almost like walking on sand with the crunching of ice particles, so it appears as if we will have an extra heavy frost.* (26 June 1954)

Robert knew that his parents would be curious about Canberra and probably sceptical of his poetic version of the city. Practically, he also realised that a car was the only real way to experience the 'natural' beauty of the landscape. He was keen to convince his family, writing to suggest that *[y]ou must come to Canberra and see it for yourself preferably when I have my car licence and can drive you around for that is the only possible way to see anything of the city. It is so countrified for even in the centre of the city there are rosellas.*

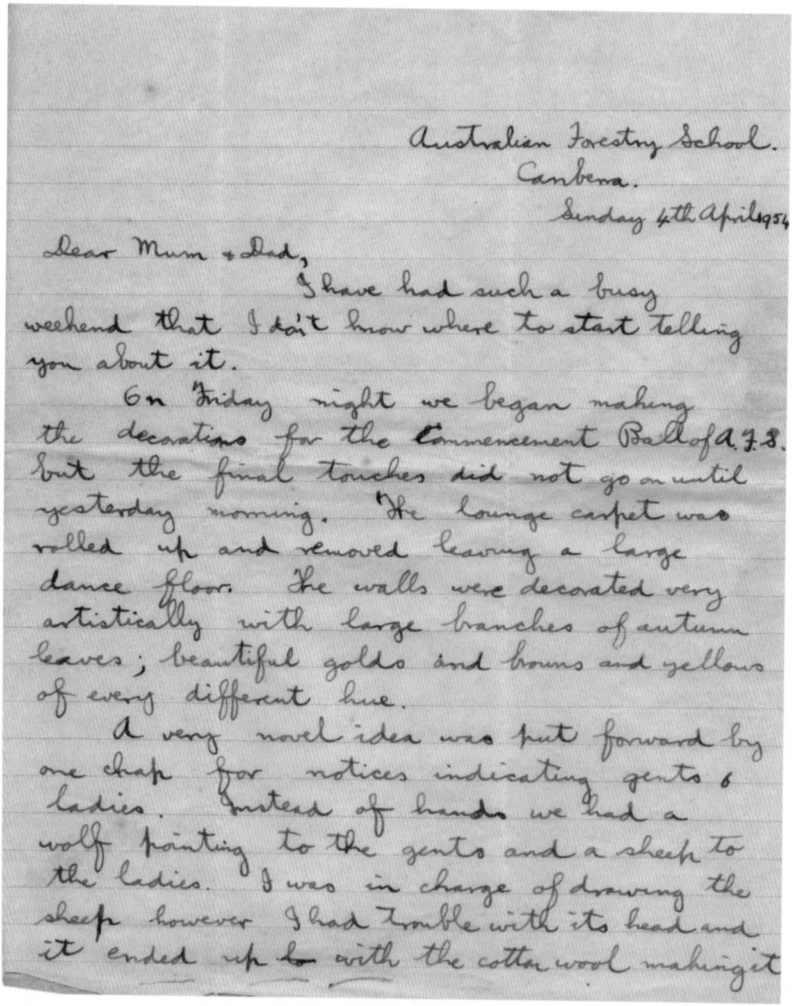

Australian Forestry School.
Canberra.
Sunday 4th April 1954

Dear Mum & Dad,

I have had such a busy weekend that I don't know where to start telling you about it.

On Friday night we began making the decorations for the Commencement Ball of A.F.S. but the final touches did not go on until yesterday morning. The lounge carpet was rolled up and removed leaving a large dance floor. The walls were decorated very artistically with large branches of autumn leaves; beautiful golds and browns and yellows of every different hue.

A very novel idea was put forward by one chap for notices indicating gents & ladies. Instead of hands we had a wolf pointing to the gents and a sheep to the ladies. I was in charge of drawing the sheep however I had trouble with its head and it ended up ~~to~~ with the cotton wool making it

11.2 Letter to Robert's parents, 1954.

'World recognised'

Robert was aware of forestry and Canberra as part of a national and international post-war modernisation project. While grateful for his foundation undergraduate study in Sydney as 'something only a university could give', he was keen for practical education and proud of the 'world recognised' (13 March 1954) standing of the Australian Forestry School. Its focus on the economic and social benefits of timber production was important to him and, in 1963, he would travel to India and Pakistan as a Colombo Plan adviser, taking pleasure in 'the profound interest shown in Australian forestry by Indian foresters', who were keen to make better use of eucalypts, 'this versatile genus'.[13] While not yet motivated by conservation, Robert agreed with the ideals of stewardship that were being promoted by his lecturers, especially the Adelaide-born and Oxford/Dresden-educated Dr 'the doc' Max Jacobs. Robert was always modest about his intellectual abilities, so the sense of possibility for his future is striking in those early letters. He wrote that

> *. . . the importance and future of forestry receives a lot of stress. We are dealing with work which definitely has a future and one of national importance. For instance we were told that at present there are 286,000 acres of timber in Australia whilst to fulfil our needs at least 1,000,000 acres are required. The job of doing this or at least supervising will be for myself and my contemporaries. With this important fact I feel certain that, if I have the ability, there will be a good position for me somewhere in the plantation, tree breeding line.* (undated)

From the perspective of 2013, it is hard not to envy the untroubled confidence with which he envisaged the larger national venture of which he would be part.

Beyond the nation, and for all his political naivety, the world was also close to Robert on a daily basis. His year had '2 Indians, 2 Malayans, 3 Ethiopians, a student who has recently come from Csechozlavakia [sic], about 5 from New Zealand and about 17 from all other states of the Commonwealth' (13 March 1954). While Bill Brown was carefully monitoring Australia's very tentative accommodation of cultural diversity in race and skill, Robert was experiencing the openings of an international world of education and expertise that would remain with him.

He became close friends with Telahun Yohanis, an Ethiopian student who was from a prominent African political family and also received support to study in Australia from a Food and Agriculture Organisation scholarship. Robert expressed reservation about Australia supporting foreign students, writing that 'It seems a bit tough to me that, indirectly through the UNO [United Nations Organization], Australia is paying these students so well whilst leaving its own on the dole, or almost' (13 March 1954). But he could see from the long nights of study, which Telahun needed to keep up with the colloquial and scientific language of lectures, that financial support was not enough in itself.

As a young man, Robert's world was mainly Anglo-Celtic and, to a much lesser extent, European. He had not left Australia, nor been to the majority of its states. Telahun, by contrast, was from an influential family and from a country whose emperor, Haile Selassie, traced a lineage back to King Solomon. He was exotic, and the ever-curious

Robert overcame any theoretical resistance in the interests of a genuine friendship. When Telahun took him to see a ten-minute United Nations documentary on the unification of Eritrea and Ethiopia, Robert was struck by the high regard in which Emperor Selassie was held. But when Robert suggested that one of their lecturers 'strutted about like Haile Selassie' (26 June 1954), Robert also noted that his friend was deeply offended, if only on his emperor's behalf.

Robert's personal and intellectual worlds expanded in Canberra. He developed a broad knowledge of world flora, scientific frameworks of understanding and practical skills. He was becoming aware of political institutions and Australia's place in the world. While he would later come to a measured view of his participation in the spread of eucalypts in Asia, as a trainee forester he saw exciting potential in early research work in the area of regeneration:

> *We were doing work on buds this week and the methods by which a tree recovers from fire and found that it is virtually impossible to kill a Eucalypt by burning in fact it increases its capacity for growth.* (undated)

Beyond these practicalities of forest management, and the signs of a fresh engagement with Australian environmental and ecological management (and mismanagement), there was something about the magnificence of trees that had captured a deeper yearning in him. Trees were big and steady. They endured and, by paying close attention, something of a tree could find its home inside a person. 'Dr Jacobs,' Robert wrote, 'is forever emphasising the magnificence of trees and tree growth and when you begin to study closely it really is magnificent' (undated).

The sense of change in Robert's letters is optimistic and achievable. He was both being educated and trained for opportunities that existed and to solve problems that seemed able to be resolved by effort and good intent.

'I might end up living in Canberra'

As early as the March in his first year in Canberra, Robert scented a trail for his future. The young man who nearly did not attend university wrote to his parents impressed by the '. . . mauve-blue gown with three black bands on each arm' (28 March 1954) of Dr Jacobs' doctoral robes. 'University Education in a Scientific Age' had been the opening address to the largest ever Australian & New Zealand Association for the Advancement of Science Conference, held at Canberra in January 1954—and, as a university city centring on but extending beyond the ANU, the promise of education pervaded many of its small social circles. It was part of a sophistication opening to Robert, which was new to his generation if in ways that seem quaint today. From Canberra he courted and married a more cultured wife, Anne MacDonald, and his sensibilities expanded. Though he was always 'Bob' to his family, and his parents 'Mum and Dad', he broached more formal relationships in his letters. 'Dearest Mother and Father,' he wrote on 11 April 1954: 'Thank you for your letters which I received yesterday'. But his claims for a more formal relationship didn't last long. The cosy always winning over the cultivated, he undermined his gains in personal protocol by immediately noting '(I liked the Robert at the beginning of yours, Mum)'. And he signed off 'Bob'.

Early in his studies, Robert began to see the 'promise of a continued and even increased demand for workers in this field' (28 March 1954). As he experienced the city, he began to comment on houses and unbuilt blocks of land that could become available—even given the long waiting lists associated with such allocation. A low score in an identification exam of conifer species by their cones caused him to feel 'disgusted with myself' (5 May 1954). He determined to study harder. By July, he was confident enough to unsettle his parents with the news that Canberra, then a five- to six-hour drive from Sydney, was likely to become his home. 'I realise,' he writes, 'that you will not probably like the idea of my working in Canberra but for the type of work I want to do Canberra seems to hold the greatest opportunities . . .' (27 July 1954). Perhaps to soften this news, he also added that 'I am sure that for anyone who wanted the bright lights and did not like gardening, Canberra would be terribly dull' (undated 1954).

Robert was beginning to settle. His stars, like those that he saw in the night sky, had become 'sharply defined'. 'Somehow,' he wrote, 'I have a feeling that I might end up living in Canberra' (undated 1954).

'An ideal city'

Robert's 1954 Canberra overlaid Walter Burley Griffin's 1912 design. These two cities touched at points, if with unsettled dimensions. Robert would have struggled as a young man with Griffin's metaphysics, but he recognised the horticultural achievements of Weston in taking Griffin's visionary but rigid plan and planting it with sensitivity in a harsh environment. As a young man, Robert was trained by foresters who followed Weston's belief in scientific experimentation and selective breeding; he worked under Pryor, who adapted Weston's formal associations to a more extensive massing of plantings, appropriate to fill the spaces of the city that followed Holford.[14] Trees needed to be tested for real conditions and considered for the full range of their amenity—visual, horticultural and productive. Canberra's streets, parks and reserves were the outdoor laboratory for Robert and his colleagues. Their focus was not on Griffin's plan, nor would they have likely considered it in much detail, but this would later change.

As Robert's career continued, he largely left experimental fieldwork for more senior positions, including with the newly established Commonwealth Department of the Environment and Conservation after 1973. Bill Brown despaired of 'multiculturalism' as a policy, but Robert became responsible for significant national negotiations in species conservation and the handing back of land in the territories to Aboriginal peoples—again, this was the role that government from Canberra began to assume by the 1970s. He began to appreciate how difficult it could be to reconcile big visions with resource management. Then in 1979 he was appointed inaugural director of the Australian National Botanic Gardens. There his interest in Griffin increased. With maturity and a sense of his own bigger field, Robert understood more of the 'frustration, marginalisation, bad luck, bad timing, and even failure' that had dogged Canberra's first architect.[15]

In 1954, Robert told his parents that

> *I should say that another twenty years will see a vast improvement for by then all the trees which have recently been planted will be well on the way to maturity and the parks and gardens will be completely laid.* (undated)

Robert stayed more than twenty years and saw a city grow. Until his death in 2009, he tried to protect the work of Canberra's 'urban foresters' of whom he always claimed to be just one. His 'magnificent trees' were his motivation, but it was important to see them in their wider associations for him and his time.

There are points in all our lives that catch us at the start of who we will become. Robert's letters take us to that point in his life. Beyond them, however, he determinedly shared his experience with many others who came to Canberra and shaped the city. These settlers were advantaged by resources and freedom from local precedent. Many worked with people and buildings while he worked with trees, but the connections were there nonetheless. The 1950s shapers of Canberra didn't talk much about Griffin, but when his star rose again in the 1990s, his vision was not lost on them. Griffin wrote in 1912, 'I have planned an ideal city—a city that meets my ideal of the city of the future'. For Robert, that ideal was not one to be reclaimed in a heroic form from the past, but captured at a more human scale in the relationships built around it. As it has been for us, each generation will need to find its own balance between the hero and the human.

Robert continued to write letters for the rest of his life—to family, friends, colleagues and government authorities. Just before his death and suffering with a loss of capacity, he was still able to draft a letter to the *Canberra Times* criticising the practice of attaching signs to trees with metal spikes. This practice could provide a pathway to infection and Robert had, as a young student, witnessed the death of a colleague when an unseen metal spike sheared off as a large tree was being pruned. The subject might seem narrow, but in its quiet insistence is the care, method and practicality that was his character and contribution. With no reference to his later academic qualifications or Australian honour, he signed it as he always saw himself and we see him through his 1954 letters:

Robert Boden, Arborist.

Notes

1 Senator Garry Humphries, *Canberra Times*, 1 September 2009.

2 See Eric Sparke, 1988. *Canberra 1954–1980*, Australian Government Publishing Service, Canberra, pp. 5, 20, 38–42.

3 Senate Select Committee on the Development of Canberra, 1955. *Report*, Australian Government Publishing Service, Canberra, p. 16.

4 Paul Reid, 2002. *Canberra Following Griffin: A Design History of Australia's National Capital*, National Archives of Australia, Canberra, pp. 244–5.

5 See Chapter 10, this volume.

6 Sir Robert Menzies, 1970. *The Measure of the Years*, Cassell, London, p. 144.

7 Hugh Stretton, 1970. *Ideas for Australian Cities*, Griffin Press, Adelaide, p. 124.

8 G.J.R. Linge, 1975. *Canberra: Site and City*, Australian National University Press, Canberra, p. v.

9 William Brown, quoted in Gwenda Tavan, 1995. *The Long, Slow Death of White Australia*, Scribe, Melbourne, p. 166.

10 See John Dargavel, 2008. *The Zealous Conservator: A Life of Charles Lane-Poole*, UWA Press, Perth, pp. 194–204.

11 Kylie Tennant, 1945. *Ride on Stranger*, Sirius, Sydney, p. 245.

12 Senate Select Committee, *Report*, pp. 16, 32.

13 R.W. Boden, 'Eucalyptus in Indian Forestry', *Australian Forestry*, vol. 28, no. 4, 1964, p. 241.

14 John C.G. Banks and Cris L. Brack, 'Canberra's Urban Forest: Evolution and Planning for Future Landscapes', *Urban Forestry and Urban Greening*, vol. 1, no. 1, 2003, pp. 153–4.

15 David Dolan, at http://www.griffinsociety.org/Introducing_the_Griffins/significance.html: accessed 4 January 2013.

12

RECOVERY STORIES

Andrew MacKenzie

When we think of natural disasters in Australia, we think of floods and fires, particularly in the last decade. Many suburban Australians have had their ordinary lives inverted by the forces of nature. I haven't tried to calculate how many survivors of natural disaster there are in the outer suburbs of Australian cities, but they must number in the thousands. Their stories involve slow recovery and they don't happen in isolation. Long after the camera crews have left, the residents go about the mundane daily practice of recovery. Their activities shine a lens on what we, as a society, deem necessary and practical in the face of adversity. Cleaning up, making insurance claims, renovating or rebuilding the home lost to the elements, purchasing the goods and services required when returning to a normal state of everyday life. These people are not looking for an idealised past to recreate, they realise very quickly that this cannot be achieved. Instead they are looking for stability, predictability and whatever constitutes normal. For many, the process of recovery is a mix of opportunities to remake a new home and life and the costs of dealing with constant change.

•

A decade ago, Saturday, 18 January 2003 was a particularly hot and windy day, so we took our three kids to the parks near Lake Burley Griffin. They were primary school age and new enough to Canberra to still find the National Triangle a novelty. To escape the heat and entertain three irritable children, we ventured into Questacon. Questacon is an intriguing building—it is designed to focus your attention inward like a vortex—however, on the top floor facing south is a small meteorological display including an anemometer perched outside an elegant observation dome. On that afternoon it was spinning so fast it looked like a propeller on full throttle—the sky was also a strange burgundy colour and rapidly changing. It's strange when you look back on what you were doing and saying that day; a bushfire of this proportion was not even within our consciousness. Leaving Questacon and wandering towards the lake we watched as the burgundy morphed into a sooty deep gray and moved eerily towards the magenta Australian flag anchored to Parliament House. As we watched the flagpole, rigid and horizontal from the force of the wind, the charcoal sky on the west of the pole slowly engulfed the clear blue to the east. Only then did we begin to realise this was a big fire. It wasn't until later that evening, when we arrived home, that we would comprehend the catastrophic events unfolding on the western edge of the city.

All Canberrans have a vivid story of that afternoon and yet very few were forced to come to terms with the full extent of the fires that destroyed over 500 houses and permanently changed the lives of thousands. At the time I had no idea that this event would also take me on a journey of a different kind. The recovery of one community, fractured by the fires and the rebuilding of their suburb, became the subject of a six-year research project. From a researcher's perspective, the suburb of Duffy provided me with an opportunity to examine the motivations of why people build what they do and how the landscape was affected by their decisions and actions. As I began talking to the different people engaged in the recovery of the suburb, I uncovered the returning residents' stories, something that could not be quantified, but needed to be told.

In 2013, what we know about the Canberra bushfires is the subject of a fading collective memory for most of the residents of the nation's capital. In January 2013, a close-knit community of suburban residents came together to remember the events of that day and the long road to recovery that, for some, continues today. In Duffy, the suburb with the greatest loss of property, much has changed. Since 2003, hundreds of residents have left the suburb never to return. Many people did return after the fires and built new houses, but have since moved on. New families have moved in to take advantage of the supply of vacant land and to build their ideal home in an established leafy Canberra suburb. A decade later, all of the destroyed properties have been redeveloped—many more houses that survived have also been rebuilt or renovated. Like many Canberra garden suburbs, Duffy looks like a suburb undergoing renewal driven by opportunity and the buoyant property market of the 2000s. A visitor to Canberra who has no specific knowledge of the fires could drive down Eucumbene Drive on the western urban edge and see new houses built on the most desirable blocks of land with distant views to some of Canberra's most iconic landscape scenery. Damaged vegetation has been removed, houses have been rebuilt and a grassy plain, once a pine plantation, now borders the suburb.

These changes are not only a necessary part of the recovery from such a catastrophic event, but were also a legacy of a planning system and community coping with large-scale and rapid redevelopment. They also reflect the values, attitudes and practices of housing at the beginning of the twenty-first century. There are many examples of residents, architects and building designers who followed the trends evident in other suburbs undergoing renewal in Australian cities. Around the nation, the story of brick veneer cottages making way for palatial suburban mansions is repeating itself with disturbing regularity across the Australian suburban landscape. The changes to scale, form and design of new houses are significantly different to those they replaced. Not only are the houses in Duffy different to those unchanged by the fires, but the planning codes and regulations are very different to those originally designed in the 1960s and 1970s when the suburb was first built.

From an urban planning perspective, the post-fire recovery activities were expected and predictable. Over the past decade, almost 500 houses were rebuilt, old families left, and new ones moved in.

Why were the new houses so different to the ones they replaced? Why, despite an increasing environmental literacy among the highly educated Canberra population, were couples and families with one or two children going into so much debt to live in five- and six-bedroom houses? Why was the green rhetoric of the architecture planning and building community so different from the practice? Social commentators identify a culture addicted to affluence, or what Clive Hamilton refers to as 'affluenza'[1]. In Duffy, affluenza appeared to manifest in the rapid reconstruction of homes by a monopolising construction industry, using pattern-book architecture and conspicuous green technologies to create equally conspicuous palatial facades. Such casual observations may support such a Hamilton-esque critique, yet the experience of the residents was more nuanced and context specific. And their experiences tell an interesting story about how the home, the garden and the suburban landscape in cities such as Canberra are valued and embodied in development practices.

•

Following the devastating fires in 2003, the community reformed and recovered as recounted in my research of two families who chose to stay and rebuild their houses. Their experiences have profoundly changed the space they inhabit, and this tells us about the flux of domestic life in our affluent consumer space called the suburb. These two families came to terms with the challenge of rebuilding and reoccupying their suburb after the fires. Despite the similar expectations of what they wanted in their new homes, they arrived at very different outcomes. Many factors affected their decision-making and design choices, but perhaps what was most evident was the way they incorporated green values into the design process. In this way, Duffy represents a microcosm of the issues facing Australian suburbs undergoing renewal in two ways.

Firstly, it reveals how the suburb has altered as a cultural space in the early twenty-first century. It highlights architecture's role in reframing the suburb from what Robin Boyd referred to as the mundane aspects of creature comforts and irritatingly austere approach to architecture, to today's pervasive view of a new conspicuous form of architecture manifested through a real-estate lens.

Secondly, it identifies how this shift—most apparent in the architecture of the redeveloped home—reflects our increasingly tenuous relationship to the suburban landscape and our conflicted approach to improving our environment through green design. It reflects on the consumers' experience of redevelopment and provides an insight into why Duffy, in the early twenty-first century, reflects the changes occurring in Australian suburbs undergoing renewal.

Since 2003, new houses in Duffy have doubled in size while the average household population decreased to just over two people. Today, the average floor area of new houses exceeds 120 square metres per person. In 1972, the average number of residents per household was closer to four and the average floor area was about 150 square metres. While the austere cottages originally built in Duffy were inadequate in thermal comfort, design quality and size, the nearly two-fold increase in floor area far exceeds the functional requirements of the residents today. I wanted to find out why back yards, no longer used for playing games or growing vegies, are deemed surplus to our needs, indeed a drain on the city's limited water resources. Yet filling back yards with spare rooms that are rarely occupied is deemed environmentally sound.

To place these events in time and space, we should consider the political and economic circumstances at the time. In January 2003, Canberra was in the grip of drought and midway through another summer of water restrictions. Yet, for most, the environmental hardship was not matched by economic hardship. Today we can reflect that this time was at the end of a long boom, not seen in Australia since the end of the Second World War. Since 1992, Australia had enjoyed a strong and continuous rise in real net national disposable income per person. Politically, individual wealth was seen as the most significant indicator of national wellbeing.

However, new interpretations of wellbeing began to attract public attention in the face of growing global social and environmental inequality. Global Non-Government Organisations such as the World Wildlife Fund and World Economic Forum promoted additional aggregate indicators for wellbeing such as ecological footprints and sustainability indices to challenge financial indicators, such as gross domestic product, as a nation's measure of wealth. This emerging interest in these measures of prosperity resulted from increasing efforts by researchers to understand the ill effects of unprecedented wealth, over-consumption and its consequences for our environment and society.

While the fetish of consumption became a popular topic of debate in some circles, it was certainly not a topic of mainstream media. On the other hand, climate change was, and quickly became, a major policy issue as Australia's population remained divided between the sceptics and believers. In response to emerging scientific evidence of climate change impacts and rising utility costs, state governments began to incorporate more restrictive development and planning policies in order to limit energy and water consumption with a view to future resources and climate uncertainties.

Canberra was one of the first cities to adopt design standards to meet the future challenges of energy and water restrictions. As a result, redevelopment and housing trends in Canberra provide a wealth of data to test the success of these policies. Today, we can look at Duffy through a number of lenses to discover what has occurred in the decade since the fires, and these results will tell of a seemingly incomprehensible mismatch between the houses built and the needs of the people who live in them. We wonder about the profound reconfigurations of the suburban landscape and the subsequent social consequences to families as the gardens and back yards are replaced by third garages, rumpus rooms and media centres.

Recovery stories

In 2010, Bryce and Margi were recently retired with adult children. When they rebuilt their house in 2004, the kids were in high school. They had not lived in the suburb for a long time but they did like the area and the neighbours. Sadly, their home was destroyed by the 2003 fires.

Bryce and Margi returned to Duffy after the fires largely because they had an opportunity to rebuild from scratch. They, like most residents, didn't arrive at the decision to rebuild as a deliberate life choice, yet when they decided to proceed their decisions were dictated by the need to invest for the future and return to a stable suburban life.

These circumstances influenced directly how their development would occur. Equally, advice from architects, building designers, planners and builders, as well as financiers, friends, real estate agents and the mass media would shape how their house would be designed and built. Residents like Bryce and Margi approached the recovery process in a fragmented way. They had created a wish list for their new home; not only to give them and their children spatial autonomy, but also to accommodate extended family that may visit or move in at some future time. The design of the home became a collection of component parts that made up a whole—only fully realised on completion. It required significant negotiation with the planners and their neighbours to fit the new home onto the block of land.

Andrew: What did you want in the new design?
Bryce: Energy efficiency—it's reverse brick veneer glazed everything. Orientation, we didn't want air conditioning, we wanted windows in the right place to catch the breezes in summer. We had a wish list as well; we wanted a craft room, a woodwork space for me. We had planned to go up to utilise the view. We also had a typical Aussie back yard with the full force of the western sun and clothesline in the lawn. The architect said you've never been able to utilise this big back yard, why don't you add this bit onto what was your backyard and shorten your back yard, which was useless space in terms of aspect.

Their architect promoted the virtues of efficiency. Her design was an effective use of land complete with efficient design interventions, green technological inclusions and high-performing materials. Even the external appearance of the home looked environmentally sound. Yet as a whole, these green interventions often underperformed and, as a result, Bryce and Margi did not think of their house as comfortable or spacious, but rather as satisfactory and functional. I interviewed Bryce and Margi on a sunny but cold June day. The in-slab heating was on but it wasn't very effective, and the blinds on the northern windows remained closed because of the glare. We sat at a table in the centre of an open-plan living room. It was covered with the flotsam and jetsam of their post-career hobbies. The remainder of the house was very clean as if it was waiting for a photo shoot. We went on a tour of the house after the interview—but we didn't view the whole house as some areas were occupied by the children, or remained empty, rooms yet to be given a use.

Two rooms at the back of the house on the second floor contained small bedrooms each with an en suite and a single bed made up with matching covers, in waiting, to be occupied by elderly relatives. We finished outside in the back yard, where the owners hadn't finished building a retaining wall to hold back the last of the old lawn, a strip of overgrown grass three metres from the back fence. Slabs of concrete pavers led to a clothesline in the corner. The owners were slowly working around the perimeter of the house to finish off the garden themselves because they had run out of money.

Margi and Bryce did not feel the landscape on their block had any value. To them, the back yard was wasted space, unusable and a constraint on their capacity to build their dream home. Yet, they had built a house for many people—there were five bedrooms, hobby rooms and vacant rooms for relatives who hadn't moved in—and children who were in the process of moving out. They did not enjoy the experience of rebuilding and it had not finished when I arrived. However, it was not at all a case of misfortune and bad outcomes. They were aware of the green technology used in their home, even though not all green inclusions met their expectations or delivered the efficiencies they had hoped for. They were, however, conscious of the appearance of their home from the street. They felt that their house was innovative and pushed conventions about what a home should be. I had a sense that their status in the suburb had improved, although at a significant financial cost. At almost 400 square metres this was a very large house. It was typical of the sort of house sociologists, ecologists and epidemiologists typically attribute to significant social and environmental costs to the suburban landscape and is symptomatic of our conspicuous consumptive ways of living. Yet it remains to be seen whether this type of home is part of the aspirations of a generation of homeowners from the long economic boom. It was clear that this sort of home could only be afforded through the significant financial commitment made by the owners and reflected the general affluence of the times.

> *Margi: With the original plans we had decided to go up, she [the architect] suggested when we go back we could also go up and have an extra room and I said 'good we can make it in to the office space', which has been great but it's a huge room which I guess is a good selling point because the house is just about an embassy residence now at least five, six bedrooms and so it's a huge one to clean.*

Bryce and Margi's home typified the normal approach to rebuilding in Duffy. Their story tells of a couple coming to terms with the tradeoffs between cost and opportunity for change, and reflects on the process of resettling into their home and suburb.

In contrast, Angela's story of replacing a home destroyed by the fires in the same suburb challenged many of the accepted assumptions about opportunity and the dream home. Her story is a nuanced relationship between her own values, the architect, her home and the community. Angela's story suggests the focus should be to find other ways to understand the relationships between individuals in the redevelopment process in order to find a better pathway to a more sustainable development outcome.

Angela lived with her partner and they had no dependants living at home. They had lived in the Weston Creek area for many years and only recently returned to Duffy prior to the fires. Angela had previous experience renovating homes and was adamant that she wanted to help design her new house after the fires. She settled on an architect only after visiting a sample of his work at a project home display village. Her focus on the rebuild was to get on with resettling as soon as possible, and in a house that demonstrated the thermal and spatial qualities she was looking for. During our interview, she didn't describe the building but focused more on the relationship and development of trust built up between herself and the architect. Her desire to include green technology was not particularly high but she was clear that she wanted the house to perform well. Angela's decisions about how her home operated incorporated discussion about both the outside and inside spaces. To this end she treated the landscape as integral to delivering the qualities she wanted in her internal living spaces.

> *Angela: Well, first it faces north, I've lived in north facing houses before and understand how comfortable they are. It is single level, it has a lot of light and a lot of space so every design decision wasn't difficult for me because it was about what would give me the most light and the most feeling of space. It looks like a suburban factory. It's grey, it's got a lot of metal cladding above wall level. It's got a bit of an industrial look to it. This is certainly more striking in appearance [than the old home], not that anyone can see it because I've planted so many trees and bushes on the west side. I'm out there every day. If it's got insects I'm spraying it, if it's got nutritional problems I'm feeding it, if they just fix the drought it would be fine.*

Angela adopted a holistic approach to re-establishing herself in the suburb. She was clear about the spatial qualities she desired. She considered the size of individual rooms, the relationship of the house to the block and how it would affect the landscape character of her suburb. She was not judgemental of her neighbours' homes, but rather critical of the approach they took in suspending their own recovery and their lack of ability to control the process or outcome. Angela demonstrated a level of command over the design process that allowed her to articulate what was important. To Angela, a light, spacious home surrounded by plants that helped regulate the visual, thermal and light qualities of her living spaces was of upmost importance to help her to recover her place in the suburb. This holistic approach to redevelopment enabled her to take advantage of the skills and aspirations of her architect. They achieved a shared vision through a process of engagement rather than necessarily focusing on the component parts of the home or allowing green credentialism to drive the relationship between herself, the design and her architect's own vision.

However, like many residents who thought of the house and landscape as deeply interrelated, Angela identified the landscape as a space where she could develop her own sense of place and identity, be it a garden, a street or the forest on the edge of the suburb. This desire for a balance rather than the planning codes determined the size of the house and how it occupied the surrounding landscape. It is true that Angela's house was not typical of most houses built after the fires. It wasn't substantially bigger than the cottage it replaced. It was designed well and achieved high environmental performance standards, and the garden formed an integral part of how the house related to the block and the street.

Angela: I love the light. I love the space. It is slightly bigger, not much maybe ten square metres, than the previous house, and it is very nice to live in. I tried to save space by not having too many cupboards because after the fires I didn't own anything and in a way, in an odd way, I didn't mind not owning anything. I mean there are family heirlooms, but this freedom of not having the burden of all this clutter and ownership was quite nice and I didn't intend replacing it. I would now like more cupboards but at the time it was my mind set that I was never going to need it.

I recently re-read Robin Boyd's fiftieth anniversary edition of *The Australian Ugliness*, and it puts these stories in an interesting historical context. Boyd argued the design of houses represented the tension that residents and designers negotiate when seeking 'a perfect balance between, on the left, the human emotional requirements, and on the right, the rational intellectual theory of building'[2]. These stories are not about the perils of conspicuous unsustainable development. They uncover the search for human emotional requirements and rational intellect as they negotiated the competing demands of their families, their community and their suburb recovering from the fires.

Maybe we just notice the big houses more, although the evidence from this research would suggest that this is not the case. However, I don't believe consumers demand such conspicuous over-sized structures, or have an aversion to retaining a back yard. Nor do I believe architects and building designers actively design custom-built homes to deliberately squeeze the life out of the suburban block, leaving a ribbon of green around the periphery. Yet a persistent phenomenon exists in society that highlights a gap between the rhetoric of good house design and development, and what happens on the ground.

Green homes not green gardens

So why does it matter if houses far exceed the needs of the occupiers? Surely the industry benefits from manufacturing, selling and constructing the additional walls, slabs, roof tiles and the associated labour going into their construction. The designers marginally benefit from the increased portion of the total building going towards design and contract management fees and the owners hope to recover the costs of their investment in the house they partially own and partially occupy.

From a broader urban perspective, such development—however logical it might seem from an investment perspective—shines a light on an otherwise illogical repositioning of the landscape in a time when architects and urban planners are struggling to explain how to make our cities more resilient, more liveable and more adaptable. Ironically, by adopting a green technological approach to urbanism, architecture and planning, the landscape has been pushed to the margins. This is in part a failure of the built-environment professions to embody landscape values in the decision-making process. The 'disappearance' of the back yard is a symptom of this changing focus. Tony Hall argues that this profound reconfiguration of the suburban landscape is a product of a move away from a home-based lifestyle and the associated time pressures.[3] However valid these socio-cultural explanations are, it does not explain why landscape values are not factored into building design let alone subdivision planning. Over the past century, many case studies exist around the world that have achieved much higher housing densities and retained significantly higher quality landscape spaces.

Examining the changes to the configuration of the landscapes in Duffy gives a more detailed picture of how these shifts in development practices have impacted on the suburban character of our cities. Many of the advocates for denser, more compact cities don't take into account the value of the suburban landscape in this way and, as a result, the size of houses continues to grow, and the corresponding blocks of land continue to shrink. Understanding new and better ways to redevelop suburbia requires a stronger understanding of how we inhabit the suburban landscape.

In Duffy, the survival stories have unfolded slowly over the past decade. The process of rebuilding Angela's home took a year and the reappropriation of the spaces inside and out occupied her life until the last paver was put down and the final tree was planted many years after she returned to Duffy following the fires. Angela has adapted to her new circumstances, but she laments the inability of her neighbours to do the same by responding to the challenges of survival. I suspect the lesson from her experience is that surviving and thriving after a catastrophe is an opportunity to re-imagine a new suburban life that includes a new suburban landscape. The fires that caused this change became secondary to the multiplicity of decision-making and pragmatics concerned with establishing a way to recover.

Angela was lucky as she had an experience of renovating, and she had a spatial brain. Her way of dealing with the catastrophe was to turn her life into a project. In the end, she was happy with her circumstances. Others like Bryce and Margi weren't so fortunate; they were stuck in a temporal void, unable to make decisions, yielding to the advice of professional designers to make the most of their block and build as big as they could. Some of these residents went into considerable debt and, by their own admission, now use only a small portion of their rebuilt house and less of their garden because, in the end, their house changed but their daily life, their rituals and practices, remain largely the same. Many people haven't adapted well because they are still traumatised by the catastrophic fires, but that is another story.

Acknowledgement

This story is dedicated to all the residents of Duffy who invited me into their homes to tell their own recovery stories.

Notes

1 Clive Hamilton and Richard Denniss, 2006. *Affluenza*, Allen & Unwin, Sydney.

2 Robin Boyd, 2010. *The Australian Ugliness* (50th anniversary edition), Text Publishing, Melbourne, p. 297.

3 Tony Hall, 2010. *The Life and Death of the Australian Backyard*, CSIRO Publishing, Melbourne.

13

REPRESENTING THE NATIONAL CAPITAL AT REGATTA POINT

Robert Freestone and Margaret Park

The city was in the process of being dressed. It was the early 1960s and national institutions, memorials, bridges and roads were in construction phase underpinning the city that was to be. The ancient Molonglo riverbed and floodplain were being refitted into an ornamental lake. Positioned overlooking this waterway, on a graded slope at Regatta Point with a vantage point designed to oversee the whole creation, was a lookout. Situated on this lookout was an unusual twelve-sided polygonal building, somewhat less imposing than its monumental surroundings, but every bit the ornament in the landscape envisaged by British planning guru William Holford in 1961. The early intent was to create a restaurant for visitors to casually enjoy the spectacle of the lake and parliamentary area.

But the impending March 1963 visit of Queen Elizabeth II seeded another idea: housing a temporary exhibition to distil the very essence of the city—its town-planning modus operandi. The building, its role, its contents and its immediate setting have changed since then but the promotion of the national capital ideal remains alive and well. In 2013, while the celebratory focus is on the city as a whole, what is now called the National Capital Exhibition celebrates its own golden jubilee.[1]

What began as the Regatta Point Planning Exhibition has been a staple of Canberra's public relations and information infrastructure for almost half a century. It has been the site of numerous official visits and events, hosted hundreds of thousands of tourists, and accommodated regular busloads of schoolchildren and other visiting groups. Without the aura of Parliament House or the awe of the Australian War Memorial, it has become one of the most enduring public institutions of modern Canberra. Most Canberrans and visitors would recall their first experience viewing the city model, reading the information panels, taking in the audio-visual display in the theatrette, and viewing the central national area from within or without.

The combination of the carefully conceived and controlled internal display alongside the more natural and free-flowing external environment proved an effective instrument for the National Capital Development Commission (NCDC) in convincing the public and the politicians that a new capital city was a benefit and a blessing for all Australians. NCDC Chief Commissioner John Overall was adamant that it was important 'to get the message out to Australians that worthwhile development was occurring in Canberra—and it was something they should be proud of rather than jealous about.[2]

Acknowledging the time-honoured power of visual display enthroned by Scottish planner-advocate Patrick Geddes as the key to effective propaganda, the NCDC had already mounted modest displays in office foyers during its early peripatetic existence in Civic. Regatta Point was a step up as a prestigious location easily accessed in a rapidly automobilising city.

13.1 Visiting school students enjoy the interactive display at the National Capital Exhibition.

As its golden era commenced, the NCDC was short of neither power nor resources but was consumed by the political and public-relations need to validate its mandate. The pressure to always be in the good books and to maintain a good standing with the powers that be in Canberra and beyond was paramount. Canberra-bashing was an established national sport and, with major building works afoot, the NCDC wanted to ensure that the nation's return on investment was seen in the best possible light. This set the scene for an extensive and sustained public relations campaign embracing publications, films, lectures, promotional events and materials, city tours, lookouts, visitor goodwill, and touring exhibits. Regatta Point easily morphed into the propaganda machine. Overseeing the production, installation and refurbishment until 1972 was the NCDC's PR man, Tom McKernan, a career journalist with a retail background.

The idea to build a viewing station in time for the royal visit was handed to NCDC chief architect Gareth Roberts. Dubbed variously 'an exhibition kiosk' and 'observation building', the Regatta Point facility was designed to be the first of many tourist kiosks dotted around strategic Canberra vantage points. It was conceived with ease of construction in mind and a degree of flexibility to be transformed from temporary exhibition space into a restaurant with a view. Detailed design work was contracted to Fowler, Maclurcan and Mansfield, later to make more of a mark with the Treasury building (1970) on the other side of the lake. John Mansfield worked quickly with Roberts and working designs were presented to the Commission in early December 1962. By late February 1963, the quirky dodecagonal kiosk was well on its way to completion in time for the Canberra Day celebrations.

Up and running as an exhibition kiosk, but devoid of refreshment rooms, kitchen, or even toilet facilities, the intention was that once the exhibition closed within a few months, the building would be fitted out as a high-class restaurant with views to match. But the exhibition took over. The Queen's visit had inspired the Commission to showcase its planning philosophy, design expertise and construction abilities. It proved a hit with the general public and within a couple of months visiting hours were extended. McKernan was in his element in transforming a temporary use into a permanent fixture on the lakefront. The exhibition in Civic was closed and Regatta Point relaunched as a tourist attraction. Herewith was the means to present the dreams of the past, the action of the present, and the designs of the future for the nation's planned capital city. Alternative sites were considered from time to time including Mount Ainslie with Robin Boyd mooted as architect in 1969. But Regatta Point maintained its appeal. What better place was there in all of Canberra to encapsulate the dynamics of the new city under construction?

13.2 The Queen visits the National Capital Exhibition on the royal tour, 1963.

In the wake of the Queen's visit came visitor curiosity—the desire in all of us to have a stickybeak—and the NCDC now had a tangible way to tap into that inquisitiveness. Any mention of transforming the building into a restaurant was robustly quashed. Many events were staged in close proximity and this brought increasing numbers of visitors through its doors. More royal tours followed, the Queen Mother in 1964 and the Duke and Duchess of Gloucester the following year, all bringing attention to the NCDC's work. Heads of state and associated delegations visited, chaperoned variously by senior politicians, commissioners and staff. Long lists of VIP visitors are recorded in NCDC annual reports. These types of visitations were usually followed by media entourages again placing the exhibition in the limelight. Wives of politicians and senior heads of departments would play a crucial role in promoting the national capital role of the city. During a 1981 Commonwealth Heads of Government Meeting retreat, the spouses of heads of state were shown around by Tamie Fraser, wife of the Prime Minister. According to Gordon Shannon, an NCDC staffer on duty: 'Tamie Fraser knew as much about it as we did and she handled the visit expertly, without any input from us. We were absolutely stunned at her knowledge and ability to manage the occasion.'

Regatta Point became an obligatory, if not the very first, port of call for countless domestic and international tourists. In the 1970s, the NCDC's External Relations section strongly advocated it as a 'place of education not only for the public but also for its own staff'. New planning strategies and publications were launched there. School excursions became big business. An internal 1981 report observed that nearly 60 per cent of school groups visiting Canberra for one night attended the exhibition. John Overall observed the significance of schoolchildren's visits to the exhibition. It was his belief that 'the best way to get parents there was to first have the children visit on school excursions and have them work on school projects concerned with Canberra's development'. He felt that children were by far the best ambassadors the NCDC could have and that as a result of their visits they 'saw more of what was happening in Canberra than many politicians'.

Visitor numbers grew steadily, up to around 200 000 visitors a year by the early 1970s. The bicentennial year of 1988 saw bumper crowds totalling well over 300 000. Even after the official demise of the NCDC, under the auspices of the new National Capital Planning Authority (NCPA), Regatta Point was ensconced as one of the most visited national institutions. In 1989, the exhibition won the prize for Best Tourist Service awarded by ACT Tourism. Annual visitor numbers climbed to over 350 000 by the late 1990s. Popularity had a downside and complaints lodged with exhibition staff centred around issues of lack of parking, buses obstructing access routes, overcrowding in exhibition areas and the theatrette, car break-ins and other acts of vandalism.

The larger role assumed by the exhibition at Regatta Point drove major upgrades and refurbishments, which in turn attracted still more visitors. The first major refurbishment didn't take place until the mid-1970s. Approaching its twentieth birthday the following decade the building was soon in need of a second major facelift. A trickle of funds had incrementally enabled display panels, models, audio-visuals and other accoutrements to be upgraded, altered, repaired and maintained. But these bandaid measures were showing signs of distress. Staff were equally under duress. The audio-visual equipment regularly failed, the model required constant cleaning, and the whole exhibition needed a complete redesign to accommodate new developments. During 1984, the facility was closed for some months to undergo a complete revamp, inside and out, resulting in the addition of a food kiosk, proper toilet facilities, enlarged exhibition space and an increase in the capacity of its theatrette. The building's new look, complete with heavy screening and a Colorbond cladding encasing the structure, detracted from the original simple lines. Nevertheless, the results provided the modern inclusions and comforts expected by the discerning visitor. After its reopening in December 1984, visitor numbers jumped by 25 per cent. The NCDC must have felt that this justified the reported $800 000 expended, although some local politicians were scandalised by costs 'out of all proportion to the need'.[3] The Commission's commitment to the exhibition was unwavering in spite of political criticism. According to one former staffer Daryl Powell, 'the NCDC was devoted to it . . . it was part of the system'.

The third major redevelopment was completed by the National Capital Authority (NCA) in November 2000 and involved a modernisation makeover and integration with a new commercial events centre for the ACT government. Reflecting a markedly changed political-economic environment, this extension was driven by business and trade interests, led by the CanTrade Board, seeking better conference and exhibition facilities. For some Canberra residents, these changes resembled what Prince Charles said of the National Gallery extension in London: 'a monstrous carbuncle on the face of a much loved and elegant friend'. However, the planning exhibition received its usual overhaul, the external 1980s cladding was removed, returning the building to its original form and patterning, the retail space was expanded, and terrazzo artwork featuring a graphic interpretation of Walter Burley and Marion Mahony Griffin's plan for Canberra's central area was incorporated into the forecourt area.

From its inception the exhibition housed at Regatta Point was always intended to evolve. Although a static display in a museum sense, it was tied in with the planning directions shaping the city. At its core was a large physical model of the city that remains even today a centrepiece. In the early years, staff would use a pointing stick to highlight key sites, a military metaphor that no doubt appealed to the ex-military commando Overall. The model was impressive for the time, perhaps as memorable an introductory marker for Canberra as the Australian War Memorial's dioramas. It needed to adapt quickly, however, as new buildings and amenities appeared. It increased in scope as Canberra's new towns of Woden, Belconnen, Tuggeranong and Gungahlin took shape. As technology improved so did the model and the exhibition: push buttons and lighting enabled visitors to see more clearly where current works were underway or where future patterns of growth would emerge. As the computer age arrived, touch screens and other whizz-bang trappings appeared. In the late 1970s, diodes were added and synchronised to include a brief commentary with slides spotlighting key elements in Canberra's national area. But staff were increasingly frazzled by the maintenance, dusting and updating constantly required.

Attempting to keep abreast of new hi-tech audio-visual aids and add an enticing entertainment factor to any Regatta Point visit, the NCPA introduced 'Cyclops' in the early 1990s. Possibly a world first, 'Cyclops' was mounted on a mast at Mount Ainslie but operated by remote control from Regatta Point. Visitors could direct the camera to sweep through the Canberra landscape and snap an image as a souvenir.

The age of gimmickry and enticements had arrived, but with this came technical difficulties as well. Weekly staff reports regularly comment on 'Cyclops' having broken down again or being confusing to operate. A fibre-optic laser display was introduced around the same time and updated for the opening of the renovations and extension building in 2000. Outmoded by the mid-2000s, this 'sound and light show' was improved and the NCA's new planning strategy was showcased in a model linking the city's planned future and its relationship to proposed works in line with the Griffin Legacy project.

Space and financial constraints have always presented a challenge to exhibition refurbishment and replacement. A major renewal was mapped out in 2009 with the exhibition designers intending to fine-tune the exhibition and provide more detail in exciting and thematic forms, with modern technology to match. Visitors would be better informed about what it means to be an Australian and why Canberra was chosen for the national capital. However, implementation has been shelved with NCA spending priorities needing to be reshuffled to accommodate more pressing infrastructure needs elsewhere, notably urgent repairs to Scrivener Dam. The idea of all-of-a-piece comprehensive renewals every decade or so has had to be rethought; consequently the NCA is moving more towards a philosophy of targeted 'rolling renewal'.[4]

Exhibition content has always been intended as an information portal, a gateway to fostering and promoting understanding of the development of Canberra. The NCDC's intent was to appeal to the general public, but also to sharpen the focus of its political masters as well as to nullify its critics, locally and nationally. It was intended as a tool, an enticement for all visitors to the burgeoning city, but significantly a resource for the new resident, the transferred public servant, and the visitor to Canberra as the harbinger of future tourism trends. Not forgotten were the international visitors and the professionals. Its central location and unique position overlooking the lake and Parliamentary Triangle would offer all visitors to the exhibition opportunities to view works in progress, to find directions to other places of interest and to learn about the role of the NCDC and the building of a new national capital.

Primitive though it must have been in the early 1960s, the basic exhibition panels and the monumental central model were of sufficient interest to keep the visitors coming and galvanise the NCDC's views on developing an exhibition to which succeeding agencies have

13.3 Heavy snow on Regatta Point in 1965.

retained a commitment. The NCDC envisaged the early exhibition as incorporating all aspects of its works from engineering to landscape design. Housing and suburban development formed a large part of the initial display and afforded an added incentive to new residents to view their own neighbourhood plans and even spot their homes and gardens newly unveiled. This not only presented the way things were or what was to come, it also was seen as helping to instil a sense of pride for local citizens forging new lives and careers in a fast growing city. Content evolved as the city expanded and new metropolitan and district planning strategies were released.

While Regatta Point may have been a useful resource for locals in its earliest incarnation, its value as a medium for exchange of local planning information was soon overtaken by its tourist function. The NCDC was open to feedback. Tom McKernan's PR team came up with the idea of distributing reply-paid business cards for visitors to express satisfaction or to make constructive criticism. By the end of the third year of operation, the feedback was informed with few shallow comments and little criticism that was 'foolishly destructive'.[5] The NCDC firmly believed that by improving and evolving its own planning exhibition in synch with the times, it was also involving the community in the planning process. Yet the basic flow of information remained one way, and within the new ethos of participatory planning from the late 1960s—a fraught period for planning agencies nationally if not worldwide—the traditional exhibition format was limited in its usefulness.

But by then it was already apparent that the NCDC was shifting the emphasis away from town planning towards a broader understanding of Canberra as the national capital for a wider audience. With self-government from 1988 and the introduction of a dual planning system, the NCPA was required 'to foster an awareness of Canberra as the National Capital', and the NCA has been obliged to continue that focus. The 2009 master-planning process called for a strengthening and refurbishment of the exhibition around three major themes: Canberra as a national capital choice, the Griffins' and later plans for Canberra, and the symbolic Canberra role and the nation's aspirations.

The original brief for Regatta Point was dedicated to an appreciation of the planning and design of a developing city. This has endured but has been complemented by a broader educational ambit covering the larger historical, symbolic and political roles of the national capital and national government. This function had been vital given what former NCDC commissioner Tony Powell sees as the 'fragility of the national capital idea' in contemporary Australia. All the while this metamorphosis has been underlain by a striking shift towards the touristic promotion of Canberra as a place to visit and experience. The building and rebuilding of the original kiosk along with the refurbishment and replacement of exhibitions over five decades provide a unique window into the representation of the national capital to the wider community and its undoubted planning heritage. Moreover, it is a place for which literally millions of people will have their own memories: popping in on a road trip, shuffling through as part of a school excursion, a *de rigueur* visit with the in-laws, attending a special event, having lunch, or just taking in the view and parkland setting.

The changing political and, especially, the economic backdrop of the exhibition have presented challenges. Resources have always been constrained and the usual trade-offs, compromises and delays have influenced the standard and content of changing exhibits. The old

Department of the Interior was constantly trying to wrestle away the 'exhibition kiosk' for it to manage and lease, which was the department's normal pattern for national capital assets. But the NCDC resisted, and the exhibition kept on keeping on, with periodic relocation plans also coming to naught. The most recent threat of the neo-liberal age came in 2011 when Dr Allan Hawke cast a critical budget-minded eye in an independent review of the whole of the NCA's operations. He regarded 'fostering awareness' as the most subjective and discretionary of the NCA's statutory functions and one that might be hived off to another agency. One scenario for doing that was to close Regatta Point, lease the space to a commercial tenant, and have visitors gather information solely from the internet. The savings were estimated at $0.7 million per annum. Hawke correctly surmised that such a move might not be commonsensical and, further, could be 'construed as short-sighted and mean-spirited in the lead up to the Centenary of Canberra'.

So happily this essay is not an obituary. Other world cities like Beijing and Shanghai have massive urban-planning exhibition halls. Twentieth-century planned cities are unevenly serviced: Brasília's underground Espaço Lúcio Costa is a desultory interpretive space which, if anything, diminishes rather than enhances appreciation of that city. Within this context Canberra's National Capital Planning Exhibition at Regatta Point more than holds its own as a place to visit; it is certainly unique in Australia.

In one sense, the place remains a throwback to a post-war context which celebrated the exhibition, Patrick Geddes-style, as a communicative instrument for planning and design as positive forces to shape modern life. Exhibition culture suffused the NCDC public relations style of the time. Into the early 1970s, the flagship exhibition at Regatta Point was complemented by several other types of 'show and tell': small-scale exhibits in suburban districts mainly for the benefit of prospective and new residents; interstate exhibitions in accessible locations to reveal the city and its progress to business interests, relocating public servants and the general public; purpose-designed exhibits for major trade, professional and parliamentary events; and major travelling exhibitions taking the idea and achievement of Canberra onto the world stage. The NCA has recently resuscitated the peripatetic show with a small exhibition on the federal capital design competition of 1911–12 showing in Melbourne then Adelaide through 2013.

As Alan Hawke contended, 'information-rich internet resources' might in some ways do the job of informing and educating the community just as well. For over a decade it has been possible to visit Regatta Point virtually through the NCA's website. The ability of traditional display panels, physical models, and even sound and light shows in this day and age to capture the imagination and at the same time to deliver information richness is arguably limited. There are exciting possibilities available through the use of new digital technologies.

For now the place itself in real time and space is special in its own quintessentially Canberra kind of way; a small but integral part of the city's national capital heritage. It occupies an outstanding panoramic site, albeit readily accessible only by car (very Canberra), and still attracts upwards of 150 000 visitors a year, almost half of them free and independent travellers. The Regatta Point Exhibition has been knocked around by major physical changes and extensions, possesses an earnestness that some have always found a bit uncool, delivers information content that others might contest as an accurate representation of Canberra as a place to live, and can struggle to get the right balance between its education/tourism roles. But it is a little Aussie battler—a survivor—with a sturdy resilience in striving to move with the times. National planning authorities from the NCDC onwards have stuck by it, too; indeed it is the only site actually owned and operated by the NCA for its own purposes in Canberra. It's been an integral cog in the Canberra experience for half a century; the city—our national capital—wouldn't be the same without it.

Notes

1 Research for this essay has ranged widely across annual reports, official publications, archival records held at the NCA, the ACT and National Archives and various histories of Canberra. Many generous informants and assistants provided their thoughts, opinions and help via conversations and correspondence including: Richard Clough, Jim Conner, Seona Doherty, Mike Grace, John Gray, Yvonne Heslop, Vin Kane, Christine Logue, Duncan Marshall, Terry Millar, Shannon Mortlock, Pamela Owen, Daryl Powell, Tony Powell, Gary Rake, Gordon Shannon, Melanie Skinner, Leisa Stack and Keith Storey.

2 John Overall, 1945. *Canberra: Yesterday, Today and Tomorrow*, Federal Capital Press, Fyshwick, ACT, p. 49.

3 Philip Castle, 'Regatta Point Exhibition Centre Costs $800,000', *Canberra Times*, 6 December 1984.

4 Gary Rake, email, 10 September 2012.

5 T.J. McKernan, oral history interview conducted by Mel Pratt, OH 645, National Library of Australia, 6 February 1978.

14

DECOMPACTING THE CITY

Jack Lydiard

In 1913, one entry and two Americans declared that they had designed the future capital of the Commonwealth of Australia—an ideal city—a city like no other. Canberra began as an aspiration in the minds of the Founding Fathers of Federation. Look forward one hundred years and the question remains: Is the Griffins' plan still looking for a city—and when Canberra enters its one-hundredth year will it be looking for a history? All the stories, narratives and architectural gestures—from the grand visions in the Parliamentary Triangle to the humble govvies swallowed by towering iron barks and blue gums lining suburban streets—tell stories of a city looking for a generation who think of Canberra as their natural home. Perhaps in 2013, we might be surprised how many young Canberrans feel this way. That, however, is a story about the past; this monograph looks to the future.

Here is the scenario:

It is the year 2113, the Canberra Centre's last retail outlet closes as the information economy finally restructures urban infrastructure—so much so that shopping, once seen as a form of entertainment, is now an online experience and other forms of recreation drive the *producer* economy. The costs of driving to and parking in the city are so prohibitive that the only people who buy goods in Civic are the locals.

The Civic locals were once wealthy retirees from the baby boomer generation—now long gone—and the high-rise apartments are occupied by the third- and fourth-generation Canberran students and young professionals who have moved from their home 'towns' to live among their own kind. They are not wealthy cashed-up individuals, but rather renters choosing places to live based on very different criteria to their grandparents. The RACCS (Republic of Australia Capital City State), formerly known as the ACT, never discovered the city behind the plan in 2013 and, in the subsequent years, Canberra has become a coalition of six towns based on the once parodied Y plan.

In 2013, the most provocative debate of the centenary year—sparked by a novel competition to rethink the city—was the perceived threat to the suburban way of life by the planning authority's urban consolidation policies. By 2023, this fear evaporated as the city–state and the federal government finally released the extensive foreshore land around the urban lakes to residential development and the noughties generation fled the depopulating suburbs in search of a meaningful living experience of town life. This concentration of citizens around the lakes and town centres developed a powerful sense of connection to place as they rediscovered their affirmation for community living. This produced a tipping point where the suburb soon became extinct as we once knew it.

Chief Minister Gallagher's parting gift to the Canberra community in 2020 was to hold a referendum to decentralise the ACT government and establish local councils around the town centres—soon to be known as just 'towns'. The referendum was overwhelmingly successful—unlike the 1988 version—and what started as a symbolic gesture to local empowerment became the defining point where the Griffin legacy was finally put to bed and replaced unintentionally by a peculiar twenty-first century hybrid version of the Holford legacy to decompact Canberra.

The towns of Gungahlin, Belconnen, Civic, Woden, Molonglo and Tuggeranong became semi-autonomous and self-governing. Each town council was established on the condition that it agreed to the 2050 RACCS Metropolitan Plan's only principle that the towns of Canberra should be world-class examples of urbanism for the new Federal Republic of Australia. The Plan, still managed by the Federal Republic's department of National Significance and Civic Leadership, on behalf of the citizens of Australia, was asked to demonstrate how cities could meet the Federation's ambitious zero carbon emissions targets by 2110—three years before the bicentenary.

In the early twenty-first century, visionary urbanists argued that cities could become net positive supporters of human life through the creation, rather than the consumption, of essential energy, food, fresh water and ecological services. By 2030, this urban model became the blueprint for a new governance structure supported and funded by the republic and city–state governments' commitment to zero-carbon emissions for cities.

By 2023, the housing affordability crisis had become intergenerational and, for the first time in eighty years, home ownership dropped below 50 per cent in the city–state. This was not seen as a bad thing as the RACCS government anticipated this as far back as the 2013 centenary year. Within ten years of the centenary, the land-sale-driven economy collapsed and the government looked to buying up abandoned offices and shopping malls to convert them into home/office campuses to recapture the profits from development that it had long ago relinquished to greenfield developers. The architecture community, excited by the idea of actually making a genuine social difference to the quality of life for RACCS citizens, lobbied the government to refocus on the once parodied notion of decentralisation. The Australian Alliance of Architects partnered with government and the community to reoccupy the towns of the city–state to decompact the city.

The collapse of the greenfield land supply was closely followed by the fragmenting of the large housing developer companies, yet their corporate knowledge wasn't lost. Many of the brightest builders and developers reinvented themselves as small niche building companies. The first people they re-hired weren't carpenters and concreters but sociologists and anthropologists, who developed highly sophisticated models of community profiles which resulted in a dizzying array of urban forms, building complexes and modes of accommodation to meet the demand for new hybrid and fluid communities. Existentialists lived differently to pragmatists, and nihilists were attracted to very different places to the communitarians. The architects worked closely with these companies and communities to design fluid buildings that could rapidly re-form to meet the needs of the occupants. Once they were constructed, builders could reconfigure homes, even within unit complexes, within days through a highly developed understanding of design for disassembly and reassembly.

By 2063, the walkable towns had become a reality, not because of the failed ambitions of the uncomfortable planner–developer partnerships that built the peri-urban new urbanist experiments in the early 2000s, but because the cost of driving had become prohibitive. Fuel now hovers around five hundred dollars a litre and the price of new cars is prohibitive because of the embodied energy costs of manufacture, distribution and disposal. One hundred and fifty years after the great Fordist revolution, cars are once again a luxury item.

This was also made possible because of a bold and ultimately successful work/life balance experiment. The federal Greens–Labor coalition of 2026 trialled a 100 per cent telecommuting government department to improve worker productivity. In doing so, they successfully achieved the Republic government's commitments to achieving the ambitious benchmarks of the new employment wellbeing index. The former departments of treasury and climate change merged to form the Department of Economic Adaptation. The work–life model for this new agency was simple: employees would work in an office space close to their home, regardless of the department they worked for, and telecommute. The program was so successful that now defunct shopping malls were converted to public-sector campuses where employees worked in a virtual office, connected to their colleagues by cloud technology made available by the now legendary National Broadband Network. Today over 80 per cent of citizens live less than twenty minutes' walk from their workplace and less than 5 per cent of the workforce actually drive private vehicles to work.

Only the wealthiest citizens live in car-dependent, suburban estates. What was once the backbone of western cities now looks more like a strange hybrid between wind farms, market gardens and eighteenth-century picturesque English estates. The depopulation of the post-war garden suburbs went into overdrive in 2030 after the cost of commuting became prohibitive. The government abandoned public transport in favour of their strategy to repopulate the towns and the federal government's virtual campus project took off due to the overwhelming success of the Department of Economic Adaptation's experiment in telecommuting.

In 2010, the notorious urban forest renewal project was the first of many reviews by the city–state that painted a bleak picture for the future of the garden suburb. The dilemma facing the city at the time meant that the government could no longer afford to maintain the landscape as it was. But by 2020, the new carbon economy turned the low-density suburb from a liability to an asset for the city–state. The Republic signed an international biodiversity agreement to protect the last remaining biodiversity global hotspots by embedding these areas into the carbon economy. As it turned out, the twentieth-century legacy of the garden suburb combined with the still intact National Capital Open Space System to make these suburbs more valuable to the city–state as biodiversity banks than residential homes.

In the past, real estate was the cornerstone of the city–state economy, now biodiversity banking underwrites the RACCS budget. The city–state government undertook to buy back the suburban homes and a few entrepreneurial citizens re-occupied the land to capture the biodiversity benefits and use the land to supply the city's energy and fresh food. Today suburbs that were once the bedrock of Australian society are now park-like estates—places like Evatt, Curtin and Giralang are urban energy and food farms and biodiversity banks.

Paddy Pentony—grandson of a former landscape architect and founder of the EPIC farmers market—now owns what was the suburb of Kaleen. He became the first of a new breed of biodiversity and food entrepreneurs. Today his estate not only produces food and biodiversity credits for the city–state, it also provides nearly 10 per cent of the town of Belconnen's energy supply through solar, wind, thermal and sewage waste power. Today over fifty biodiversity billionaires such as Paddy are feeding and fuelling the six towns of the city–state by providing three-quarters of their food and energy needs.

Today not all is well in the 'burbs, not all Canberrans wanted to, or could afford, to leave their homes. Some of the biodiversity estates were more successful than others and residents who opted to stay in the suburbs became increasingly isolated by the complete absence of services as the city infrastructure retracted around the towns. Some communes formed and, through either choice or necessity, these people lived a largely subsistence life. Despite these communities scoring highest on the sustainability index, they were not so happy. They had given up their right to self-determination and their wellbeing index was, on the whole, very poor. The reinvigorated leasehold system meant that the biodiversity lairds could not evict these people. However, a few of the suburban residents chose to work on the estates in return for food, energy and water, education, and free access to the National Broadband Network. Ironically, these people scored higher on the wellbeing index because, for the first time in many generations, their families had managed to break the welfare dependency cycle. So the suburbs were once again subordinate—the home for the marginalised in society. In a strange fate of history, they housed the wealthiest and the poorest citizens who also happened to be the happiest and most miserable.

While the economy has radically changed, some things remain the same; people still need face-to-face contact to do business, but not all the time. The cultural institutions in the face of ongoing budget cuts have partnered with the biodiversity billionaires to build the Melbourne–Canberra–Sydney–Brisbane ultra-high-speed solar-rail network to reposition the parliamentary zone as a major national convention and education hub. Plane flights have all but disappeared and telecommuting

14.1 In 2113, Republica is a semi-autonomous province for a million-strong temporary community.

has extended into the education sector. Students, businesses and public servants embedded in the knowledge economy converge regularly on the Democracy Triangle via rail to meet face to face and to attend intensive learning studios and laboratories as higher education is replaced by lifelong education. In 2115, a world economic congress will meet in Canberra's internationally famous conference park—the Democracy Triangle—to discuss the state of the new global producer economy where carbon has long replaced cash as the monetary standard.

As education and work converge in the Democracy Triangle, so the virtual city of 'Republica' has emerged as a semi-autonomous province for a million-strong temporary community that stays in the RACCS for week-long face-to-face intensive meetings and workshops a few times a year. Unlike the other towns, the virtual city of Republica is an accident of history as a result of the warming of the oceans due to climate change causing catastrophic sea-level rise. The financial and government institutions of the major coastal cities have abandoned their central business districts due to sea-level rise. The cost of rebuilding the infrastructure along with the impossible problems of congestion, has led the major coastal cities to abandon physical centres in favour of virtual central business districts.

This has allowed the RACCS to get a jump on other cities in creating a place to conduct traditional meetings for the majority of companies that have shifted to the telecommuter business model. Even the manufacturing sector has taken over the once innovative Brindabella Park to create a twenty-four hour, mixed-residential manufacturing precinct along the eastern boundary of the city, and in recent months has made moves to create the first new town government in fifty years.

Today the built environment and planning professions have learned from their mistakes of the past. Instead of relying on grand visions, the planning authorities have collaborated to produce 'live metropolitan plans' where the city's future is rewritten daily by the events and dramas of the changing global economy. The planners are now experts at using real-time community engagement tools via the National Broadband Network to navigate the future of the city in partnership with the residents. Due to the success of Republica, more Australian citizens are also contributing to the ongoing planning and production of the metropolitan plans of the Capital through the blogosphere. New utopian fantasies that look beyond the realm of the online world are used to inspire and provoke the community to be better at producing a new urbanism.

15

STILL SETTLING THE LIMESTONE PLAINS

Stephen Dovers

Settlement unsettled

For many people, Australia was 'settled' soon after European occupation, through the actions of hardy, resourceful and sometimes foolhardy 'settlers'. These people then somehow departed the narrative of the evolution of Australian people and the Australian continent. They faded first from Sydney, which went from 'settlement' to town and then to city, where settlers do not exist. Settlers hung on longer in the bush, but there too they faded away. It seems that once the survey pegs are removed and houses built, settlement ceases. Occasionally other settlers have popped up—'new settlers' as another term for migrant 'new Australians', and 'new settlers' again but later as alternative lifestylers escaping from deviant, consumptive cities. But overall the modern era put paid to settlers, settlement and settling—these are now past tense in the public mind.

At least three things are wrong here. First, human settlement of the Australian continent began well before white occupation, at least 50 000 years before, and Indigenous settlement is an unfinished story. Second

15.1 'The Bath Room, F.C.' (Federal Capital Survey Camp), postcard from 1911.

is the presumption that the process of settlement has stopped. Third, the settlement story has largely overlooked urban Australia—cities as post-settlement phenomena, devoid of settlers. So let's unsettle the standard story of settlement.

'Settlers' as we traditionally understand the term were on the future site of the National Capital from the 1830s, and things stayed recognisably and typically rural until 1911 when very new lines began to be drawn on maps in the first moves towards a new settlement that would transform the human landscape in this part of the world, from rural to eventual city. One member of the survey team for the new capital was George Harris Sargent Dovers, my grandfather. The confirmation of Canberra in 1913 had ceremony and great import, although the physical changes were slow to unfold.

15.2 Federal Survey Camp, 1911, George Dovers at right.

Back then, and for quite a few decades after, there was a sense that the new Canberra was central to the national project of settlement. But surveyors and others were assessing and mapping the land around here well before that. Captain Mark Currie RN and his party travelled east of the district in 1823 and onto northern Monaro, describing the country as having an 'interesting nature connected to sheep grazing'. The country was open, with grassland between scattered trees, and woodlands and thicker forests on the higher and steeper ground. South of the Limestone Plains and on his way to Michelago, Currie enjoyed the view of a 'chain of clear downs'. You could de-pasture stock without laborious clearing. Why the country was open is part of an earlier human settlement that we are only beginning to understand. There were doubtless forbs and shrubs scattered there, too, and the species composition of the grasses was very different, but we don't understand much of that.

Some of the trees you can see living and driving around the Limestone Plains are relics, pre-dating white settlement by a good margin, the standing dead from another era. We don't remark enough on those structures in the landscape 300 or 400 years old, just on human-built structures much younger. People rested in the shade of some of those trees before our earliest white settlers were born.

Alongside Currie was ex-convict Joe Wild, who informed the party of the local Aboriginal people's names of places. He knew the country already, and was as much the explorer and discoverer as Currie. He served the same role with Charles Throsby, a pioneer and parliamentarian in finding a way into Illawarra where the interest was coal, not sheep. But Wild didn't write the journals. There are many unspoken and unwritten voices in the story of settlement, but the question of which European first 'discovered' here or hereabouts is unanswerable anyway—by the time Currie made Monaro there were cattle and sheep already out grazing. The official record of settlement often lags a bit behind the actual story.

Going through early journals in the archives for clues of what the landscape was like can be rewarding but frustrating. The detail is never quite as precise as we would like—the description 'the tall spiky grass' doesn't quite tell us what we want to know. Is the Kangaroo Grass that has lately returned to the landscape in fenced-off areas during drought the same species as what was there back then, or something else?

Stewart Ryrie's sketches from his wonderfully perceptive and careful survey of Monaro in 1840—they had been separated from his journal in the state library until the 1980s—show a familiar landscape of open country not far south of Canberra, with scrubby rises on the shallow soils. Ryrie's assessment of land capacity and limits in 1840 was as good as anything done for over a hundred years afterwards. Canberra is lucky in having a good stock of early writings, sketches, maps and photographs. Canberrans are startled by early photographs of Black Mountain as grassy, open woodland rather than forest.

Current research that seeks to understand our woodland ecosystems is constrained by a lack of knowledge of the pre-European condition of the landscape. I believe that the author and historian, Eric Rolls' conclusion in northern New South Wales that grass and shrub layers were transformed in a very few years after de-pasturing stock holds true in many places. The very earliest descriptions are invaluable where they exist. Rolls annoyed a few scientists and historians along the way, but was a splendid pioneer of understanding the present landscape through the past via his books such as the seminal *A Million Wild Acres* and

They All Ran Wild. Here on the Limestone Plains as elsewhere, we need more local and detailed environmental histories to inform our ongoing settlement and each place has its own environmental history.

Early accounts can correct later interpretations and assumptions. In 1835, the Austrian naturalist, artist and author John Lhotsky went south, unsupported by the usual patronage of colonial society, and by necessity had more dealings with everyday people in the landscape. His journal shifts from science and geography to sharp social observation. Sir Keith Hancock in his classic 1972 book *Discovering Monaro* described the lower reaches of the Numeralla River as a 'wreck', and many people would look at that stretch of river now and agree. But Lhotsky reported local knowledge describing the river bed as wide, difficult to cross, and featuring 'shifting sands'. We have established the chronic decline of many of our rivers, but did we transform the Numeralla within a mere decade, or are there local exceptions to the general degradation narrative?

The evidence from early journals is rarely firm. Captain Mark Currie entices us with descriptions of a haul of fish from the Bredbo River, which he describes as 'resembling the rock cod of Port Jackson'. But exactly which rock cod did they look like, and so were they more likely to be Trout Cod or River Blackfish, both now endangered fish species? Blackfish cling on, but Trout Cod may well be locally extinct in one of its last refuges on the Murrumbidgee River near Tharwa since the latest drought.

Early explorers and surveyors were very much part of the settlement story—they mapped country and divided it into owner and use. But we are still drawing lines on maps that will fashion the landscape for decades and centuries to come. New suburbs will be there a century on. So a hint of where I am heading: the Land Development Agency and ACT government planners are doing the same thing right now. So are developers and local governments in neighbouring districts. These people are part of the settlement story, just like Currie, Dixon and Griffin were on the Limestone Plains.

There is a deeper history of settlement that has been too long overlooked, and still is under-represented in the settlement story. Things have improved in recognising and paying our dues to country long settled and stewarded by Australia's first peoples, but we have yet to reach an enduring and satisfactory settlement between Indigenous and white Australia. When the *Mabo* decision came down in 1992 many of us celebrated, and felt relief from an uneasy guilt over our collective lack of recognition of those millennia of past stewardship. We could start to pay the rent, morally and perhaps even literally. The retractions and friction that emerged in the public debate post the later *Wik* decision, and much that has happened thereafter, shows that race in Australia still has potency. If the perfectly practical and not-too-disruptive instruction for negotiated regional agreements that was glaringly implicit in the High Court's *Wik* decision sent people into a panic—albeit a carefully organised one fed by deliberate distortion—what would the reaction be to genuine joint management in the more settled areas of Australia? Indigenous lands now comprise over one-fifth of the land mass, and Australia is regarded as an international model for our joint management arrangements in some national parks, and even more so for the growing estate of Indigenous Protected Areas, but the whole issue is still very unsettled.

The basis of the *Mabo* decision was that there was, and in places still is, an active form of native title, and that equalled a land with law, not the land without law that was the colonial assumption of *terra nullius*. The 1992 decision meant that we recognised the Australian landscape was one that was actively managed by people. This is a legal truth that many people still struggle with, and is the biggest unsettling of the standard white story of settlement. Aboriginal burning techniques are still poorly understood, even in places like Kakadu where we seek to blend modern science, Indigenous law and custom, and human safety considerations in fire management. Elsewhere, there will have been many different practices suited to different climatic and vegetation conditions, and we are only beginning to understand or even ask what these techniques might have been like, and whether they are relevant in the present era.

The standard story of settlement is homogenous in ways other than its very slow recognition of Indigenous stewardship. It isn't just black and white, as the recently inflamed and sharp debate over asylum seekers and immigration shows. Some attitudes now are pretty much the same as those held against the Chinese in the gold rushes, or the opinions expressed in *The Bulletin* in the late nineteenth century.

Settlers in suburbia

Another gap in the standard story of settlement is that it is usually related as non-urban, which is strange in one of the world's most urbanised societies. The Australian urban population exceeded the rural population well before the end of the nineteenth century. The bush and rural myth has been a minority experience for three-quarters of our post-occupation history, but ever powerful.

Cities rarely feature in the standard story of Australian settlement. Urban Australia in the story of white settlement has been mostly an aberration or an apology. Recall A.D. Hope in the poem 'Australia':

And her five cities, like five teeming sores,
Each drains her: a vast parasite robber-state
Where second hand Europeans pullulate
Timidly on the edge of alien shores.

Canberrans can at least pullulate at a distance from the edge of alien shores, safe from sea-level rise. Cities have been often viewed as unnatural in the standard story of settlement—teeming sores indeed. From the 1820s clear visions were expressed of the preferred society that Australia should become, and it was overwhelmingly rural—the sturdy yeomanry doing morally sound work on the farm and living in what was proposed to be 'frugal prosperity'. I have always wondered what exactly was meant by frugal prosperity, but I suspect today's farmers and pensioners may know.

Whatever one's idea of the 'real Australia', whether city, suburb, town, paddock or bush, all are real and they are fully interdependent. The city–country divide is a political and media artifice mostly, but it has its roots in the settlement story. Most constructions of our 'heartlands', in TV documentaries, books and research programs, place the heart of the country inland or in the arid centre. In the outstanding book *Australian Heartlands*, Brendan Gleeson provides a political, demographic and economic antidote and puts the heart in the suburbs. The cultural, economic and political heartland of Australia is suburbia, even if precious intellectuals and stoic agrarians might not see that. Are we still settling the suburbs? Bloody oath we are.

Canberra is a peculiar part of the Australian settlement, a mix of national symbols, well-spread suburbs and bush setting. From a shared vision of nationhood, the term 'Canberra' has become almost an insult. Many Australians have been conditioned by populist, stupid commentary from politicians and media and, as a result, have lost pride in a shared national capital.

Still settling

So millennia on, Australians of all sorts are still settlers and are still settling the Australian landscape, that place that Eric Rolls described as confronting the white occupiers with 'more a new planet than a new continent'. Cities hide the raw biophysical difference of Australia more than little towns and farms; they mask the immediacy of environmental variables; and material and energy trades and flows camouflage locally unsustainable patterns of settlement. But we are still settling Australian urban landscapes in this peculiarly Australian process of settlement.

There is another problem with the settler myth—its individuality. Even back then, the mostly white and male, hardy individual settler of the standard story of settlement was not so individualistic. He was supported by public subsidy, early irrigation systems, government survey, railways and roads, national development agendas, immigration assistance, convict transport, closer settlement schemes, and land grants. Settling Australia has never been entirely individualistic, or just government-driven, or privatised, or community-organised, but a mixed bag. Strong government intervention has always been part of the story: the Robertson Land Acts in NSW were remarkable in their attempt to break the squatters' power; irrigation development was a very public exercise; the state built the railways and funded research and weather stations for national development.

The challenges of governing settlement shift over time. Are the challenges of change and settling greater and quicker now, as many claim? That may well be wrong, and is certainly a fruitless line of thought. In any relative sense, the pace and scale of changes in human settlement in the past was challenging—post-war urban growth, revising production and consumption in city and bush for wartime production, provision of universal access to clean water and schooling, the impact of the car and telephone, shifting global commodity markets, the advent of universal artificial lighting, and so on. Were these somewhere lesser changes and challenges, relative to institutional and technological capacities, compared to our agendas now? Probably not, and who cares anyway? Each era has challenges and deals with them intelligently and fairly or not.

The last thing wrong with the standard story of settlement is that it stopped well in the past. Settlers were then, not now, or even recently. That's wrong as the story is ongoing, and I think we can comprehend our past, present and future better if we accept settlement as a continuing and fascinating story that we are still part of. We are still settling the Limestone Plains. And not just on the Limestone Plains. We are still settling Australia, and we are still settling cities and towns as much as the farm and the bush. Subdivisions are settlement, as is tree planting in country or city, densification through housing form, discovering something new about our soils and climate, putting in domestic water tanks and solar panels, unearthing minerals, building power stations, fencing, or erecting public artworks. It isn't just the big players who are fashioning the landscape for the future, who are essentially settlers, it's the farmers, builders, scientists, landscapers and the owners of back yards too.

Resurrecting the term 'settlement' repositions current debates in a long story of interaction between people and place, of learning and legacies, of deliberate and accidental change creating the future. The process of human settlement imposes change on land and on people, and is impacted by other drivers of change. We are not anywhere near to being settled in our relationship with the Australian continent, or fully capable of comprehending and handling the factors that influence us, which have not varied as much over time as many imagine—climate variability, resource availability and scarcity, our political institutions, demographic change, trade flows and shifts, and so on. In fact, we are as often unsettled as settled.

It took almost three decades after the First Fleet to figure how to remove eucalyptus stumps to allow cultivation—burn them!—and we have been experimenting with the Australian environment ever since. Still settling as we build, learn, progress, regress, and plan and create human landscapes. It is apparent that we have yet to show that we know how to build dwellings or plant gardens suited to the Australian meteorological and hydrological environment. Look at any new suburb.

In a water-scarce land, we use massive quantities of high-value, treated water to shift faeces. Our rebates, educational programs and restrictions do not really address the world's highest per capita water demand, which is structured into our cities and behaviours. We can't even tell if those policy interventions work because the data is not made available to allow proper analysis. Unbelievably, in a country where water is so critical, it is only now that we are building what might be a proper, ongoing system of data and knowledge about water resources and use and other critical urban stocks and flows. I repeat *might be*, as we have taken our hands off the wheel before. Our understanding of groundwater is in deficit.

South Australia saw a celebrated case of settlement exceeding advised limits of climate, when people moved across Goyder's Line late in the nineteenth century, and learned hard lessons in an unsettlement where people left the landscape. We talk a lot about the impact of climate and drought now. And we have fears that parts of the landscape will be unsettled through intolerable heat or lack of water. Such unsettlement is happening now as small communities wither at the end of stranded irrigation assets as water markets have their logical impact. In cities, those who cannot afford to live in increasingly costly urban environments that have been created by deliberate policy interventions are unsettled, and others settle there instead. On the coast to the east of Canberra, younger locals move inland because the houses near the water are being snapped up by investors from the city.

Does that sound familiar from a deeper history? Various closer settlement schemes starting with the Robertson Land Acts of the 1860s have left a very recognisable mark on the landscape, even now when the too-small parcels of land have been merged or lie scattered but under common ownership. That era was full of unfair and disruptive speculation and peacocking of land too. A combination of deliberate policy decisions and poorly considered actions around housing over the past few decades have had massive impacts as they—very predictably—transformed the housing market in a way that will leave lasting legacies in the style, demographics and spatial location of housing in the Australian landscape. Pat Troy in his 2012 book *Accommodating Australians* ends with the statement that 'the light on the hill was extinguished some time ago'.

The closer settlement story is still with us. We have had decades of unresolved argument over the issue of protecting agricultural land from urban expansion and non-commercial recreational farming on small lots. It is more profitable to let it go, but will we later regret the attrition of the agricultural base? Peri-urban agriculture occupies around 2 per cent of productive land but produces over 20 per cent of economic return. Can we run an agricultural system and feed the people from pony clubs and cut flowers? The economic efficiency imperative behind water markets is forcing water use towards forms of production that use less water and produce more dollars. But as someone recently said, you can't feed the country on chardonnay (but, of course, you can live on shiraz).

Australians have very different understandings when it comes to what logic should underpin our public decisions—equity, long-term sustainability, a desirable future landscape, short-term profit? It has always been thus, but the ongoing direction of settlement is I think now more obviously unsettled by fundamental ideological and practical differences that are blurred and confused in the populist, instant culture of politics and media. That is simply a result of living in a much fuller world, with less room to move and compromise, and more room for conflict. There aren't many empty spaces to move into.

There is another form of closer settlement policy being both debated and implemented in Australia—densification of our cities. Concerns over transport, spread of suburbs, and claims that denser cities are more liveable and efficient are pushing us upward rather than outward.

Many of the claims on the benefits of denser, multi-storey housing need much more support from proper data and analysis to become convincing. But, more importantly, we have demonstrated the ability to make both dense and sparse cities environmentally, socially and economically unsustainable, whatever the actual relative merits. We are obsessed with poorly evidenced debates over urban form (density) and ignore the critical matter of urban structure and strategic, long-term planning, in Canberra and elsewhere. And we will live with the consequences of that for a long time.

The Limestone Plains now

What decisions are we making now that will shape the Australian settlement in twenty or fifty years, and shape Canberra? Or in one hundred years: I would congratulate Canberra Museums and Galleries for staging a speculative 2113 exhibition for the centenary rather than a party or post-mortem. And are we thinking forward about the decisions we are *not* making now? We have made decisions in the past which shaped the future landscape, but we have also not done things and that can be just as fateful. This allows some what-if speculation.

Canberra is the product of past decisions. The location of the nation's capital was in part rational assessment, but also political wrangling and judgement. It could have easily landed somewhere else and the Limestone Plains would never have become Canberra. The national capital might have had another name. Some other design than Griffin's could have won. With the decision on location and plan, it was inevitable that this landscape would end up with the highest density of research capacity per capita and per hectare than anywhere else.

What an incredible resource. The Limestone Plains are very well known and understood following years of ANU, University of Canberra and CSIRO staff and students and other researchers using it as their local laboratory. That is a strong foundation for an ongoing, well-informed settlement and the resulting data could be better used.

Further afield, the high country was transformed by the Snowy Mountains Scheme, another part-rational, part-political decision. That has determined the river flows in south-east Australia, and forced close attention to Alpine ecosystems, and that did much to develop the crucial science of ecology in this country. But it could have been different. Had the politics shifted, the alternative option of a big dam on the upper Murrumbidgee at Billilingra might have been the result, and Canberra and Monaro would be a different places.

The great Australian historical geographer, Joe Powell, identified the pivotal role of foundational environmental knowledge as we tried to come to grips with plants, animals, climate and hydrology that defied British expectations. We are still seeking and assembling foundational environmental knowledge in a chase to inform decisions that we have to make, or think that we should make, and to make them in time.

Closer to home, we need to understand how our own environment works. Grassy box woodlands are the dominant form of vegetation in Canberra and these woodlands have been much changed, and are endangered. On the edge of the expanding suburbia of Gungahlin, there is the Mulligans Flat–Goorooyarroo Woodland Experiment with a predator-proof fence containing world-class ecological science.[1] In a partnership with the ACT government, CSIRO and others, led by my ANU colleague Adrian Manning, research has created the opportunity for us to really understand what woodlands are, and how they can be restored. The re-introduction of the locally extinct Eastern Bettong, as a likely 'ecosystem engineer' is the attention-attracting tip of the scientific iceberg. The 'Bush Capital' can become not just a slogan and backdrop, but an informed merging of humans and nature. But such research lives off serial short-term funding. The Ecologically Smart Bush Capital is a fragile and partial thing. The notion of Australia as a 'clever country' is best represented in the deeply clever ways in which our plants and animals adapt and prosper in this strange, variable environment.

How will people relate to such a world-class effort in conservation and active research right on their suburban doorsteps? Can Canberrans and nature really co-exist when we get serious and scientific about conservation in an urban setting? In a partnership with the Land Development Agency, the Fenner School of Environment and Society is adding social science to the mix to explore that question.

Why just at Mulligans Flat? Why not a future where more parts and aspects of Canberra and the Australian Capital Territory are well-run, long-term, active experiments informing smarter and smarter decisions, drawing on the immense research capacity that lives in this town? Not just a national capital, but a *national laboratory for better settlement*. That might just make a few more people see Canberra as a valued part of the Australian settlement.

The trees in protected or remnant woodlands are only part of the story, even if they have been the main focus of conservation efforts in the past. The landscapes of the grazing and wheat-sheep zones of Australia feature scattered or paddock trees in the midst of productive land use. These landscape icons are more valuable than we thought for production, and much more valuable than we thought for biodiversity—people like them, and they are dying. They are old and they are not recruiting under grazing management. What is being planted in admirable programs of land regeneration fades against the scale of the demographic decline. Vast tracts of land will be treeless in future without action.

Recent research by Joern Fischer and colleagues in the Fenner School's Sustainable Farms Project shows that the key to encouraging paddock tree recruitment—to supplement planting where there is no seed stock—is to reduce fertiliser inputs and shift to high-intensity, fast-rotation grazing, with long rest periods.[2] That is a radical departure from traditional grazing management. The implications have been investigated, in close partnership with innovative farmers who are very much still settlers. Changes in land management are being trialled with good results. Foundational environmental knowledge is still being assembled, as part of settling into this landscape.

If you look and listen closely, you can hear the inspirational stories of innovation, prosperity and sustainability that can be found on the properties of those who carefully pick and choose new management ideas to trial and to improve them amidst the pressures of reaping a living from an often unforgiving climatic and economic environment. The landscape managers to watch don't talk too loud and are not doctrinaire—so many are both—but are implementing a quiet revolution in managing Australian landscapes. They may not be recognised yet, but that is always the case. The first manager to plant lucerne in this part of the world early in the nineteenth century to balance seasonal feed fluctuations was dismissed for mismanagement.

If anyone tells you that they have a singular answer to Australia's natural resource management problems—it might be organics, natural sequence farming, biodynamics, pasture cropping, holistic management, land retirement, obsessive tree planting, whatever—then they are wrong. There are lots of answers. The landscape, the people and the different parts of the farm system demand varied answers, and we need the humility and intelligence to match the answer to the problem. The same applies to simplistic nostrums for our cities: they are far too complex for singular solutions.

In between those scattered trees is the productive base of this region's main form of primary production—the grass that feeds the sheep. In the 1920s, sand drift from rampant soil erosion covered the Monaro Highway. Landscapes were degrading alarmingly. In his work on soil conservation, legal academic John Bradman—known then as John Bradsen—summarised national parliamentary debates around the Second World War. These included statements that soil erosion would damage Australia more than the bombs that were then falling on Germany would damage that country, and many references were made to a 'national crisis'. The birth of soil conservation agencies around the country in the mid-twentieth century was a response. Those agencies have all but disappeared and soil has declined on the policy and scientific agenda. We have scarce soil resources and we are ignoring them.

But those agencies, along with research organisations and farmers, repaired landscapes in the middle of last century with physical works and especially by developing a regime of improved pastures. That involved the fertilisers that we now understand to constrain regeneration of scattered trees. The improved pasture regime is also implicated in soil acidification. The environment is a complicated thing, and one intervention will have multiple results. It took a while, but in the early 1980s Australia got its head around that complexity and focused on 'land degradation' as an interrelated set of issues including various forms of soil erosion, vegetation decline, salinity, structural and chemical change in soils, and so on. That integrated approach didn't last long and the overwhelming focus shifted to dryland salinity, at the expense of all else. Soil acidification apparently disappeared. But it's still there, a problem, and being ignored.

Large, occasional trees don't just matter in rural areas, but in town as well, as recent research has shown. The research used Canberra as its laboratory.[3] Picture a large old eucalypt tree in one of Canberra's neighbourhood parks. Canberra has over 300 of these parks, with one within 400 metres of every house, making them a fantastic opportunity to investigate the role of small urban greenspaces as habitat for wildlife, such as birds. Research has found that large old park trees are crucial keystone habitat structures, providing birds with important places to forage, nest and shelter.

We have a history of forgetting: science and policy seem only able to attend to one or a few things at a time. For example, water policy and research in Australia evidences peaks and troughs of activity that closely correlate with El Nino cycles. We forget problems when they aren't at crisis level, even though they are fundamental, like water or soils, or fires and floods. Energy is fundamental, but Australia still lacks a coherent energy research strategy and has not had a proper energy policy for decades.

Not forgetting is the theme of the National Arboretum in Canberra, a living memorial and inspirational vision arising from the horror of the 2003 Canberra fires. Former Chief Minister Jon Stanhope's vision was a bold and risky one: criticism has faded, thankfully, and the vision embraced as the trees grow and the extraordinary parkland has been created. Happily, through an agreement between the ACT government and the ANU, the arboretum will also function as a long-term research site, and is used as a field site for training of forestry and environmental science students. With a deliberate experimental design aimed at exploring climate change and the effect on tree species, it will be an even more appropriate memorial and celebration of place.

Our early settlers did things that we now regret, like channelising rivers, introducing rabbits and clearing too many trees in some places. In retrospect, these were short-sighted and often wrong decisions. But they were confronted by a strange environment, had very little data and few options in a struggle to feed themselves and create a future. We have far fewer excuses now for getting it wrong and should be careful of laying blame on the past. We have more knowledge and, in the future, we could have much more, especially in and around Canberra.

The future Limestone Plains

Some big decisions are now being made about the future, the settlement that will be Canberra years ahead, the product of the legacy of past settling and the settling we are doing now. Will that Canberra have 500 000 people? Will it be painfully and expensively car-dependent in an increasingly oil-scarce world? Will the structure of the city allow for equitable access to employment, schools and other basic services, in line with the best traditions of town and country planning? Will the unique natural and semi-natural landscapes in and around the city be well-understood, biodiverse and enjoyable, or ignored, trampled and dead? Will we agree about the role of fire in the landscape, or still be engaging in blame and attack? Will our policies and plans speak to each other, or will environment, society and economy still be treated as unrelated?

Consider an ambitious future for the Limestone Plains in the centenary year. That future may be twenty or fifty or a hundred years away, but the end point is less important than the process along the way. That future proposition is for Canberra and the Australian Capital Territory—the Limestone Plains—to be the best informed human settlement in the world, a laboratory where intelligent experiments in settling test ideas and inform the way forward. This isn't a vision of a perfect, defined state but an invitation to embark on an experiment, where we set out questions that need to be answered to achieve that goal, and then work towards it—a real long-term plan for a sustainable settlement. The next proposition is that if we can't create a best-practice human settlement here in Canberra, then we can't do it anywhere. Let's deal with the vision first, and then the capacity to deliver it.

Let's think of a future where the Bush Capital is the site of a world-class experiment in human settlement. Buildings will be efficient, and more affordable. We will have a fine-scale understanding of energy and water consumption in the city and manage those crucial resources abstemiously. The urban structure will be designed to cater for human health, access to services and employment, and efficiency, not just to maximise returns. Our various plans—for transport, open space, energy, housing, infrastructure—will be coordinated, and monitored against good, fine-scale data. The reserves and open space will be ecological laboratories producing first-rate knowledge that helps us get better and better at managing the Australian environment—right here but also informing endeavours elsewhere. The Mulligans Flat experiment would no longer be exceptional but accepted practice. We might even have a good consensus on living with fire and kangaroos—there is finally some proper monitoring of kangaroos and their interactions with our grasslands that will produce some light rather than heat.

That future Canberra would no longer be known either as a required but unexciting educational tourist destination or a symbol of dissatisfaction with politics, but a human settlement that produces intelligence, insight and lessons in how to live in Australian landscapes. How to be better settlers. There would be a different sort of national institution in the city that houses national institutions—an institution of growing knowledge with top-class science, exciting announcements to the Australian people, and more intelligent planning and management of the city. Where's the downside?

This town has many people likely sympathetic to such a vision. It has the research capacity in spades. It has the national capital status to justify the vision, and a good mix of urban, rural and natural landscapes. It is a manageable jurisdiction, a city–state with strong institutions, and a valuable merging of state and local government functions. It has an electoral system that has more (mostly unrealised) potential than most to encourage non-adversarial politics suited to collaboration and long-term planning. The 'Canberra Experiment'.

Those are all positives, so what are the barriers? I'll pick on three. The first is the persistence of silos and fragmentation, in government and in the production of useful knowledge. Departments and disciplines still operate too much in isolation, and in competition. Some of us are arguing at the moment for using Canberra as a test-bed for an integrated knowledge system to support sustainable development, connecting research capacities, policy and management agencies, and the community. It has never been done before, and it could be done here more easily than anywhere on the planet.

The second barrier is the domination of short-term imperatives and quick fixes, which are a result of special-interest power, electoral cycles, the limits of forward estimates, a media and public who crave instant gratification, and a lack of understanding of how to plan ahead in a flexible way. The third is simply that such a vision is lacking—we haven't thought about Canberra in such a positive way. That sounds like a nirvana of human settlement, a project that any settler would be proud to work on. If we can't do it here in Canberra, on the Limestone Plains, then we can't do it anywhere.

Acknowledgements

This essay is an edited version of the author's 2010 Sylvia Curley Oration, and draws together and extends arguments and material from previous work of myself and colleagues.[4]

Notes

1 D. Shorthouse, et al, 2012. 'The making of the Mulligans Flat—Goorooyarroo experimental restoration project', *Ecological Management and Restoration*, vol. 13, no. 2, pp. 112–25.

2 Joern Fischer et al. 'Reversing a Tree Regeneration Crisis in an Endangered Ecoregion', *Proceedings National Academy of Sciences*, vol. 106, 1991, pp. 10386–91.

3 Karen Stagoll et al. 'Large Trees are Keystone Structures in Urban Parks', *Conservation Letters*, vol. 5, 2012, pp. 115–22.

4 Stephen Dovers (ed.) 1995. *Australian Environmental History: Essays and Cases*, Oxford University Press, Melbourne; and Stephen Dovers (ed.) 2000. *Environmental History and Policy: Still Settling Australia*, Oxford University Press, Melbourne, and a keynote paper to the 2007 State of Australian Cities Conference.

CONTRIBUTOR BIOGRAPHIES

Kate Rigby

Kate Rigby is an Associate Professor of Comparative Literature, Monash University Melbourne. She is also a Fellow of the Australian Academy of the Humanities and of the Alexander von Humboldt Foundation.

Frank Moorhouse

Frank Moorhouse is a writer of fiction, non fiction, screenplays and essays. His most recent novel, *Cold Light*, is set partly in Canberra in the 1950s during the Cold War and the discovery of uranium. It won the Queensland National Prize for Literature and was short-listed for the Miles Franklin Prize.

Marion Halligan

Marion Halligan is a writer and novelist. Her first published short story appeared in the *Australian Women's Weekly* in 1969. She was made a Member of the Order of Australia (AM) in 2006 for services to literature and for her work in promoting Australian literature.

David Headon

David Headon is a cultural consultant and historian. He is Advisor on the Centenary of Canberra and Advisor to Senator Kate Lundy as well as Visiting Fellow at the Australian National University. David is a regular commentator on cultural, political and social issues on television and radio.

Christopher Vernon

Christopher Vernon is an Associate Professor in the Faculty of Architecture, Landscape and Visual Arts at the University of Western Australia. Chris has written extensively on Canberra and the Griffins.

Andrew Sayers

Andrew Sayers is the former Director of the National Museum of Australia and inaugural Director of the National Portrait Gallery. Andrew was awarded a Member of the Order of Australia (AM) for service to art administration.

Shanti Sumartojo

Shanti Sumartojo is a Postdoctoral Research Fellow in the Department of Sociology at Australian National University. She has a PhD in sociology and a Masters in nationalism studies from The University of Edinburgh.

David Nichols

David Nichols lectures in Urban Planning at the University of Melbourne. He has a broad range of research interests focusing on urban, suburban and regional cultures and communities in Australia.

P. Harness

Prik Harness—aka Mikel Simic and Geoff Hinchcliffe—were a 1980s art-rock band from Canberra, and were renowned for their wild stage costumes and antics. They often wore crochet bikinis onstage.

Glenda Cloughley

Glenda Cloughley is a practicing Jungian analyst, psychotherapist and musician. Glenda won a New Mythos Grant from the Opus Library and Archives Center, California, for research towards *The Ethos Epic*, a sister work to *The Gifts of the Furies.*

Susan Boden and Nicholas Brown

Susan Boden is a landscape architect with additional training in mental health. She also works as a freelance researcher and writer. Nick Brown is an historian based at the National Museum of Australia and the Australian National University.

Andrew MacKenzie

Andrew MacKenzie is a landscape architect and design academic at the University of Canberra. He has a PhD in interdisciplinary environmental studies and a Masters of Public Policy from ANU.

Robert Freestone and Margaret Park

Robert Freestone is Professor of Planning and Urban Development at the University of New South Wales. His research interests are in planning history and metropolitan restructuring. Margaret Park is a researcher and historian.

Stephen Dovers

Stephen Dovers is a Professor and Director of the Fenner School of Environment and Society at the Australian National University. Stephen is a leading scholar of environmental policy, natural resource management and environmental history.

Canberra Lab

Canberra Lab is the actualisation of the desire of a group of young architects and designers to establish a discourse within Canberra's design community. It is a platform to critique, discuss and discover Canberra's built environment and an opportunity to investigate the city and explore its potential.

CB.1 Cyclist enjoying part of the cycle path network circumscribing Lake Burley Griffin.

PICTURE CREDITS

P.1 Canberra brickworks (National capital Authority—NCA—collection)

1.1 Kayakers on the Murrumbidgee (NCA collection)

1.2 Filling lake (NCA collection)

1.3 View along Ainslie Avenue to Mount Ainslie (NCA collection)

1.4 Red Hill kiosk (NCA collection)

1.5 Furies present case for Earth (Glenda Cloughley)

2.1 Boys in britches, 1928 (NCA collection)

3.1 Marion Mahony Griffin tryptich (National Archives of Australia—NAA)

3.2 Monaro Mall (NCA collection)

4.1 Senators spying out the land at Orange (National Library of Australia—NLA)

4.2 O'Malley hitting peg on Capital Hill, 20 Feb 1913 (NLA)

4.3 Aerostation (NLA)

5.1 Parliament House etching (Romaldo Giurgola, with kind permission of Pamille Berg)

5.2 Aldo (Annette Condello)

6.1 Australian War Memorial (Flickr)

7.1 David Tolleys playgrounds, 1966 (NCA collection)